Unequal Partners

PITT LATIN AMERICAN SERIES

John Charles Chasteen and Catherine M. Conaghan, *Editors*

Unequal Partners

THE UNITED STATES AND MEXICO

Sidney Weintraub

University of Pittsburgh Press

Published by the University of Pittsburgh Press, Pittsburgh, Pa., 15260
Copyright © 2010, University of Pittsburgh Press
All rights reserved
Manufactured in the United States of America
Printed on acid-free paper
10 9 8 7 6 5 4 3 2 1

Library of Congress Cataloging-in-Publication Data

Weintraub, Sidney, 1922–
    Unequal partners : the United States and Mexico / Sidney Weintraub.
        p. cm. — (Pitt Latin American series)
    Includes bibliographical references and index.
    1. United States—Foreign relations—Mexico. 2. United States—Foreign
economic relations—Mexico. 3. Mexico—Foreign relations—United States. 4.
Mexico—Foreign economic relations—United States. I. Title.
    E183.8.M6W44 2009
    337.73072—dc22   2009052314

To my Mexican colleagues
and their contribution to my thinking

Contents

Prologue

Mexico fascinates me, and over the past thirty years I have written much about the country. My intention in this book is to ponder on the deepest aspect of the Mexico–United States relationship: that of a dependent-dominant attitude that has long colored official behavior of the respective governments. The official conduct is a reflection of the thinking of much of the two countries' populations. There have been constant changes in the behavior of Mexico and the United States toward each other over the years, but the dependency-dominance attitude has retained much power.

A ubiquitous word used by scholars who discuss this bilateral relationship is *asymmetry*. The current gross domestic product (GDP) of the United States is almost $14 trillion, some sixteen times larger than that of Mexico, at $893 billion. The per capita GDP figures in purchasing power parity terms are United States $45,845 and Mexico $12,775.[1] Mexico in 2007 sent about 82 percent of its merchandise exports to the United States. These imports constituted about 1 percent of U.S. GDP, whereas these exports represented 25 percent of Mexico's GDP. Another example of this asymmetry can be seen in the military: The United States has the world's strongest military establishment. Mexican authorities must assume that this power will not be used against Mexico, because it could not afford the cost of military forces large enough to defend against a U.S. attack.

However, *asymmetry* is not synonymous with *dependency*. The differences in economic and military power diverge in varying degrees between the United States and just about every other country in the world, but the extent of Mexican dependency on the United States is replicated in few other countries. Mexico lost half its territory to its neighbor the United States in the nineteenth century; territorial aggrandizement and proximity have shaped the mutual attitudes. Today, Mexicans migrate to the United States with the hope of improving their families' standard of living during their working lives, whereas most Americans who reside in Mexico believe their income can help them live more comfortably in their retirement. What has interested me is understanding how this asymmetry became a dependency-dominance relationship, and how it has shaped the social mores of the populations of the two countries.

In the 1950s I was stationed in the U.S. embassy in Mexico City for three years. I had never been in Mexico before, and I learned to speak and read Spanish there. My attachment to the country was enhanced when my last child, a girl, was born there. I think of her as my *mexicanita*, but she does not have dual citizenship because she was the daughter of a U.S. diplomat. The Mexican population was then and still is predominantly mestizo. Once I started to understand the country, it became clear to me that the European-origin population controlled the government, dominated the economy, and was on the top of the social hierarchy. It is still remarkable to me that an Indian, Benito Juárez, was Mexico's president for many years during turbulent times in the mid-nineteenth century. The historian Enrique Krauze has made the point that "Juárez opened the door wide for mestizos to reach commanding positions in the life of the nation. . . . Never before had Mexico been closer to a democracy than it was in this period of the Restored Republic."[2] Indeed, never before, but it is also accurate to say the country has not been closer to being a true democracy since then.

Twenty-four years after I left Mexico to continue my career as a foreign service officer, I became a professor at the University of Texas at Austin. Mexico was geographically close, and I chose the country as an important subject of research. As an economist, I focused on the socioeconomic aspects of Mexico and U.S.-Mexican relations. Proximity gave me the opportunity to visit Mexico often—the border, the capital, the business hub of Monterrey, and many other parts of the country. Much of it is quite beautiful, but the social conditions in some areas are deplorable. I tried to take it all in, write about it, and rewrite as I learned more. This book is a distillation of many key observations over the years.

I am entranced by the variety of cultures—Aztec, Maya, Olmec, and others—that has existed in the region over the millennia. My favorite museum in Mexico City is the National Museum of Anthropology, because it displays the various cultures quite vividly. Few countries can match the quantity of sophisticated paintings, sculpture, and artifacts that have been produced in Mexico over thousands of years. Mexico has become a violent country in recent years, a point detailed in chapter 4, which traces the narcotics situation between Mexico and the United States. My impression remains, however, that Mexicans by and large are a nonviolent people. The horror of the revolutionary period at the beginning of the twentieth century, and then the violence in the civil conflict that followed, have not been forgotten by the survivors of those years. Their loathing of the killings of that period has surely been passed on to their children and grandchildren. Drug trafficking is not the only cause of Mexico's current violence, but it is the dominant one—a violence that has its origin in the United States's large drug consumption.

During my years with the U.S. embassy in Mexico, the country was a pseudo democracy, an authoritarian land that went through the charade of formal elections. My initial assignment was in the embassy's then small political section, consisting of two young officers and a section chief. The campaign for the 1952 presidential election got under way shortly after my arrival. There were five candidates for president, including Adolfo Ruiz Cortines of the Institutional Revolutionary Party (the Partido Revolucionario Institucional, PRI). Everyone knew that Ruiz Cortines would be declared the winner, but the other junior officer and I decided to play a little game: we asked ourselves what the authorities would deem to be a convenient allocation of the votes among the five candidates. As I recall, we were within two percentage points of the official figures for each candidate.

The PRI, under a different name (Partido Nacional Revolucionario, PNR, or the National Revolutionary Party), had assumed office in 1929 and did not lose the presidency until 2000, when the election of Vicente Fox of the National Action Party (the Partido de Acción Nacional, PAN) was accepted by the then weakened PRI. I do not wish to delve deeply into Mexican history here; suffice it to say that there was a gradual transition from a one-party system to political democracy. There was also a movement toward a slightly different trajectory from a government-dominated economic structure to one more reliant on the market. During the 1960s and 1970s there was some bloodshed in the process, but the final shift was peaceful.[3] Today Mexico is a democracy, although there are weaknesses in the electoral processes, such as clandestine official support for candidates from the party in power and great disparities between parties in the financing of elections. In addition, Mexico's poverty and other inequalities make elections inherently unfair. However, the country's electoral irregularities are scarcely graver than those in the United States.[4]

The economic growth between 1982, following Mexico's debt crisis, until now has been only about 2.4 percent a year under a largely market-based economy.[5] The domination of the political scene and the private economy by persons of European origin has not provided outstanding performance. Mexico is an unequal society in which the richest 10 percent of the population receives 39 percent of the income; the poorest 20 percent receives only 4 percent.[6] About 40 percent of the Mexican population lives in poverty, which the World Bank has defined as living on the equivalent of two dollars a day; half of these individuals live in extreme poverty, or on one dollar a day. The greatest poverty is in rural areas. Under a program originally called Progresa and now called Oportunidades, there has been much mitigation of the effects of poverty.[7]

Educational opportunities are less available in rural areas than in the cities. Bribery is omnipresent throughout Mexico. Estimates are that about 40 percent of the working-age population works in the informal economy—sometimes referred to as the underground economy. These people pay no income taxes and receive modest government services, no social security but some health care. This recitation of Mexico's serious economic and social problems is by no means complete. These issues have captured my attention in my work on Mexico. My affection for the country continues despite its policy shortcomings, but my respect for Mexico's leaders and the society at large would be greater if underlying and structural problems were dealt with more effectively.

The United States has a large stake in Mexico's socioeconomic and political progress. If Mexico were richer, the United States would export more to it. The United States exported $6,463 of goods for each Canadian in 2007, but only $1,134 for each Mexican—the difference is a reflection of Canada's much higher per capita income.[8] The flow of unauthorized Mexican migrants to the United States will slow down in time as Mexico's population growth diminishes, but the current bilateral hassle would be much diminished with a richer Mexico. The United States cannot solve Mexico's problems, but it can help in the six areas discussed in this book: trade, foreign direct investment and finance, narcotics, energy, migration, and the border. I think most Americans would support a positive approach in relations with our neighbor to the south. I hope this work provides a solid analytical basis for such an approach.

Acknowledgments

The original drafts of many chapters in this book were prepared in Cuernavaca, Morelos, Mexico, during the summer of 2008. This placed a burden on Alaina Dyne, who had just joined the office of the William E. Simon Chair in Political Economy as the research assistant; just when she was learning how the Center for Strategic and International Studies worked, she had to be in regular touch with me in Mexico. She did both jobs well, and subsequently she helped me enormously in my research and getting the manuscript into presentable form. I am truly grateful for her dedication.

The initial grant for this book came from the Ford Foundation with the support of Cristina Equizábel, who then directed the Mexico office of the foundation. The support was most valuable, indicating that a book on how the two countries make policy toward each other was a viable project to a discerning funder.

Writing this book would not have been possible without the financial support of Mexico's largest cement company—indeed one of the largest in the world—Cementos Mexicanos (Cemex). The encouragement from Cemex's Javier Treviño Cantu, senior vice president for corporate communications and public affairs, was invaluable. He understood immediately what my objectives were in writing a book on making policy between two countries so unequal yet so important to each other. I also received help from Gregorio Martínez Garza of Cemex.

Cemex is located in Garza García, just outside Monterrey. Treviño suggested that I consult with scholars at the Instituto Tecnológico y de Estudios Superiores de Monterrey (ITESM, or Monterrey Tech, simply known as the TEC). I did so and received important support from Dr. Bernardo González-Aréchiga, dean of the Graduate School of Public Policy at the TEC (the Escuela de Graduadas en Administración Pública y Política Pública, EGAP). I stayed at EGAP for a week, and González-Aréchiga arranged many of my interviews and provided office facilities and other amenities that facilitated my productive work.

A friend and colleague of many years, Alejandro Ibarra-Yuñez, was the director of the doctoral program in the School of Business Administration (the Escuela de Graduadas en Administración y Dirección de Empresas, EGADE) at the TEC when I was doing research there. I wish to thank him for his substantive guidance and helping me set up many conversations with faculty and students at the TEC, businesspeople of Monterrey, and officials of the state of Nuevo León, where Monterrey is located. I wish to thank all of these people for giving graciously of their time and insights.

I learned much from my discussions with faculty and students at the TEC campus in Mexico City. The arrangements there were facilitated by Professors Carlos Urzúa and Isabel Studer Noguez. I also met with faculty at El Colegio de México in Mexico City and wish particularly to thank Gustavo Vega Cánovas for his comments. Gerardo Bueno y Zirion made useful suggestions for changes and additions to drafts of the initial chapters of the manuscript. Rogelio Ramírez de la O provided data I would not have found myself on many items that were sold at lower prices in the United States than in Mexico because of oligopoly pricing.

Many young people who interned for the Simon Chair did time-consuming work that enabled me to compile timelines (included at the end of the chapters) highlighting key facts contained in the book. These interns were Adam Berkland, Wamiq Chowdhury, Alaina Dyne, Ranieri Rodrigues, Aaron Seider, and Ann Stillman. Alaina Dyne and Wamiq Chowdhury were later hired as research assistants with CSIS. Two interns for the Americas Program at CSIS, Sarah McCune and Russell Prag, assisted me as well. Alaina Dyne and Aaron Seider were responsible for preparing the bibliography, using endnotes as the basis for this task after receiving guidance from two editors of the CSIS publications office, Donna Spitler and Roberta Howard Fauriol.

Two former U.S. ambassadors to Mexico kindly gave me their insights about the Mexico-U.S. relationship, John Negroponte and James Jones. So did Thomas F. "Mack" McLarty, who served in the White House during the administration of President Bill Clinton as chief of staff and later as the resident expert on Latin America.

I wish to thank Joshua Shanholtzer, acquisitions editor at the University of Pittsburgh Press, and Alex Wolfe, production editor at the Press, for the encouraging way they dealt with my manuscript. I most assuredly am grateful to two readers, one of them unknown to me, to whom the manuscript was sent. They had evidently read the draft with great care, and most of their corrections and suggestions have been incorporated into the final manuscript. My thanks also go to Amy Smith Bell, the freelance editor who thoroughly and efficiently copyedited the manuscript.

My wife, Elizabeth, was patient with me, especially during my writing in Cuernavaca. She is an excellent editor and gave me valuable guidance on word usage.

Unequal Partners

Introduction
Mexico's Political Economy

The idea the Mexican people have of the United States is contradictory,
emotional, and impervious to criticism; it is a mythical image. . . . In general,
Americans have not looked for Mexico in Mexico; they have looked for their
obsessions, enthusiasms, phobias, hopes, interests—and these are what
they have found.
—OCTAVIO PAZ, 1979

I see where we are starting to pay some attention to our neighbors to the
south. We could never understand why Mexico wasn't just crazy about us;
for we have always had their good will, and oil and minerals, at heart.
—WILL ROGERS, 1928

This book examines the repercussions of the dependent-dominant relationship between Mexico and the United States. "Repercussions"
refer to the shaping of policy initiatives by either country, the initial
responses by the other country, how outcomes have been determined and
with what consequences. On a larger canvas the dependency-dominance outlook of the two countries have shaped the attitudes and behavior not only of
governments, but also of the populations of each country toward the other.
The character of the two governments as they interact with each other has
been permeated by this sense of dependence on one side and dominance on
the other. Individual thinking that Mexico is a dependent (and hence inferior)
nation may be built into the consciousness of many Americans (*norteameri-
canos*). Many Mexicans have reached a related conclusion, mostly with little
forethought, not that Americans are superior, but that their country is dominant and consequently it often behaves arrogantly. One way of expressing this
Mexican attitude is that Americans think of Mexico as its backyard, not as
a sovereign and equal neighbor. This expression received much attention in

both countries when, shortly after he used it in 2003, Adolfo Aguilar Zinser was dismissed as Mexico's ambassador to the United Nations.[1]

This attitude of dependency-dominance has many origins. One of these is the self-evident asymmetry in economic and political power of the two countries. Many Mexicans, when they use the word *asymmetry*, have in mind such things as Mexico's dependency on the United States as an escape valve for emigration and the heavy reliance on the U.S. market for exports. However, asymmetry is a common phenomenon in U.S. relations with other countries, and global use of the dependency-dominance characterization would not be appropriate in all those instances. Mexico is a neighbor of the United States, but that reality makes *asymmetry* insufficient by itself to characterize the relationship.

Mexico, over the past 150 or so years, has suffered many humiliations from the United States. The most severe was the loss of half its territory in the Treaty of Guadalupe-Hidalgo in 1848, after Mexico's defeat in the Mexican-American War. Use of the military to demonstrate dominance or to grab territory was not uncommon in the nineteenth and early twentieth centuries; this was one way U.S. power manifested itself at those times. One can cite comparable dominance and territorial aggrandizement between other pairs of neighbors, one weak and the other strong, such as Germany and Poland and Japan and Korea. For most Americans this land grab is a footnote in the U.S. experience; for Mexico, though, it is probably the dominant event of its modern history. There have been other humiliations. One such example was the interference of the U.S. ambassador in the overthrow of Francisco Madero (the leading figure in the ousting of Porfirio Diaz) in 1913, after the Mexican revolution in 1910; this became known in Mexico as the *pacto de la embajada*, or the deal struck in the U.S. embassy. And there were the military incursions into Mexico in 1914 when U.S. President Woodrow Wilson gave orders for a naval occupation of Veracruz.[2] Indeed, the form that Mexican nationalism has taken stems from these humiliating events.[3] The Mexican mantra of "no interference in the internal affairs of other countries" stems from this bilateral history.

Octavio Paz, probably Mexico's outstanding philosophic analyst, argued during his lifetime that the differences that exist between Mexico and the United States stem not from the well-known "opposition between development and underdevelopment, wealth and poverty, power and weakness, domination and dependence," but rather from the reality that the two countries are "distinct versions of Western civilization."[4] Paz is well known in Mexico and among Americans who write about Mexico for the following ideas, among others: that people of each country have a mythical image of the other; that the history of the relationship is one of mutual stubborn deceit, usually involuntary; and that the United States is a society oriented to the future while Mexico's orientation is just the opposite, to what he calls a "plurality of pasts, all present and at war within every Mexican's soul."[5]

Paz was the outstanding interpreter of his own country's patterns of thought, and he was also informed about the United States, but some of what he described may apply to relations between other countries. The United States revels in its repeated victories—over Mexico, Spain, in two World Wars, and in the Cold War. Mexico is not the only country that has had repeated military defeats with accompanying national remembrances. Hungary and Poland may be other examples. The people of these countries take pride in other accomplishments and in their survival—not their expansion. But U.S. history is more ambiguous than these "victories" just described: for example, the United States lost the War of 1812, but that was long ago, and it has failed to come out of more recent wars with unquestioned victories, such as in Korea and Vietnam. Who knows how history will assess the war in Iraq? At the end, in an article he wrote during the Cold War, Paz asserted that the mortal danger the United States then faced came from within: "from that mixture of arrogance and opportunism, blindness and short-term Machiavellianism, volubility and stubbornness which has characterized its foreign policies during recent years."[6] Many of these observations have had validity in recent U.S. foreign policy.

History has clearly played a large role in generating Mexico's sentiments of dependency, but so does Mexico's inability to deal effectively with economic and political problems during the past thirty-plus years. These troubles have included, on the political side, the government's inept and violent handling of the 1968 student uprising and the long duration of faux democracy under the Partido Revolucionario Institucional (the PRI, the Institutional Revolutionary Party); and on the economic side, the inability of Mexico's political process to confront and resolve basic structural issues relating to tax collections, fiscal policy, the prevalence of monopolies, and corruption. This inability is covered later in the chapter.

In 2004 two Mexican institutions—the Centro de Investigación y Docencia Económicas (CIDE), a research and higher education institution, and the

Consejo Mexicano de Asuntos Internacionales (COMEXI), an independent foreign affairs think tank—teamed up with the Chicago Council on Foreign Relations, which had surveyed U.S. public opinion on foreign affairs for decades, to do a parallel study in both countries. Two important findings of that study are highlighted. The first is that 68 percent of Mexicans had warm feelings for the United States, and no other country ranked higher. Mexico ranked third behind Great Britain and Germany in terms of warm feelings of Americans. The second key finding is perhaps more revealing: 63 percent of Mexicans polled supported permitting Americans to work alongside Mexicans in guarding Mexico's airports, seaports, and border with the United States. This willingness contradicted just about everything Mexican leaders, politicians, and intellectuals had been saying.[7]

CIDE and COMEXI directed a second opinion survey in 2006 that was more expansive than the earlier survey, and added an interesting wrinkle comparing the views of Mexican leaders and the Mexican public on a number of issues. The warmth of feeling of Mexicans toward the United States rose to 74 percent in the 2006 survey, but the warmth toward Canada was higher, at 75 percent. Warm feelings of Americans toward Mexico were 47 percent, lower than toward five other countries (Great Britain, Australia, Japan, Germany, and Israel, respectively). There were significant differences between the views of leaders and the general public on some issues. One such difference was on accepting the presence of U.S. agents on Mexican soil cooperating with Mexican authorities: 51 percent of the Mexican public supported the idea, while only 29 percent of the leaders did. There were 1,499 general public interviews, and 259 interviews with leaders from government, politics, business, media, and nongovernmental organizations.[8]

Opinion surveys, as is well known, measure sentiment at a single point in time; they can be biased by the way questions are framed. Yet it is noteworthy that there was little change in the views cited on the two aspects of Mexico-U.S. relations in the successive surveys. Even at the time these extensive polls suggested that the majority of Mexicans had a *positive* attitude toward the United States, however, BBC polls taken during the same period indicated that the majority of Mexicans had a *negative* attitude toward the United States.[9] One explanation for this simultaneous contradictory evidence may be in the difference between overall sentiments (the CIDE-COMEXI polls) and attitudes on specific issues. The negative Mexican view in the BBC polls is centered on U.S. actions in the Middle East, especially the Iraq war.

One cliché describing the bilateral situation is that it is a love-hate relationship. There is a scintilla of accuracy in this characterization, but not much more: there is little hate on either side, and "love" is the wrong word. Respect for the United States exists to some extent on the Mexican side, but perhaps opportunism is a better way to put it—that is what drives migrants from Mexico. The title of Alan Riding's 1984 book, *Distant Neighbors*, captured a real phenomenon. But some 10 percent of the Mexico-born population now lives in the United States, and the kinship relations they have with families in Mexico reduces "distance" appreciably. Vicente Fox, when he was president of Mexico, often claimed these U.S. residents as part of his constituency. He was right in that many had dual citizenship, but they had no deep affinity with Fox or his political party; the affinity they had was largely with their relatives back in the home country.

Characterizations of attachment, fondness, admiration, and distance between the two countries all have validity, but only in a limited context. The Mexican word *gringo* or *gringa* started out as a way to express contempt for an American, but today the word is used just as often as an expression of affection. "Chicano," when used in the United States, is used to describe a group of Mexican-origin people with no real connotation of friendship or distaste. The Mexican media often react sharply to offensive statements by members of the U.S. Congress on the assumption that this must reflect government policy, although by now most educated Mexicans know this is not so. The U.S. system with its separation of powers permits congressional members of the party of the president to take whatever position they think their constituents prefer, regardless of the president's views. One recent example of this was the opposition of the Republican congressman James Sensenbrenner of Wisconsin in 2005, when he was chair of the House Judiciary Committee, to President George W. Bush's proposal on immigration legislation. Such opposition is rare in a parliamentary system, especially from a legislative committee chair. During the years that the PRI was in power and the Mexican legislature rubber-stamped whatever the president wanted, this was akin to a parliamentary system, and offensive anti-American statements by legislators could not be dismissed summarily as unrepresentative of the view of the executive branch. Now that the Mexican congress is a de facto independent branch of government, the situation of individual legislators is much as it is in the United States.

Both governments regularly pronounce that relations between Mexico and the United States are good. In the limited sense that there is practically no official name-calling and the two countries generally agree on issues of foreign policy, this is true. They did not agree, however, when Mexico, from its temporary position on the Security Council of the United Nations, indicated in February 2003 that it would not support a U.S. invasion of Iraq. Opposition to the U.S. invasion was widespread in the Security Council, and the United States withdrew the resolution. Mexican opposition to such a major U.S. proposal was unusual. Indeed, many Mexicans had argued against taking a nonpermanent seat on the Security Council for fear that their government would have to take positions antagonistic to the United States. This concern was a reflection of the dependency syndrome.

Specific Issue Areas

The central hypotheses of this book are twofold: (1) the belief that Mexico approaches the United States with diffidence because of its sense of dependence, and (2) that the U.S. reaction to Mexican proposals, or when the United States submits its own initiatives that affect Mexico, is as the dominant player. These hypotheses are tested in six policy areas: trade, foreign direct investment and finance, narcotics, energy, migration, and the border. Each area is important to the bilateral relationship. The argument is not that behavior on either side is static, but rather that as one goes back in time, the unfolding of bilateral policy was largely defensive on the Mexican side and aggressive on the U.S. side. The approaches changed in each area over time—Mexican positions gradually became more insistent and U.S. behavior less domineering—but the earlier habits have not completely disappeared. With respect to dependent-dominant interaction, the more it disappears, the more productive the bilateral relationship will become.

The main time period covered is from 1954, when the "Mexican growth miracle" was at its zenith, to the present. However, much attention is given to the period beginning with the 1982 debt crisis, because it was then that the Mexican government had an epiphany: it realized that whatever benefits earlier economic policies had, and these were in fact substantial, they were no longer suitable. The main economic changes after 1982 were to look outward rather than inward, to give emphasis to export promotion rather than export pessimism, to rely less on central government dominance and management of the development process, and to stress the role of the private sector and the market. One of the key manifestations of this change was the decision to adhere to the General Agreement on Tariffs and Trade (GATT) in 1986, an action that the Mexican government specifically rejected in 1980. Greater import opening and export promotion began in the few years before Mexico actually joined GATT, but the symbolism of joining the most important world trading body by a populous developing country was substantial both inside Mexico and throughout the rest of the world. Being part of the negotiating group that led to the formation of GATT after World War II was a big deal. GATT has since been replaced by the World Trade Organization. The metamorphosis of Mexico's trade policy is laid out in more detail in chapter 2.

Two areas in which Mexico has shifted from deference to public assertiveness are migration and narcotics trafficking. In 2001, in the migration area, Jorge Castañeda, then the foreign minister in the newly constituted Vicente Fox administration, said that what Mexico wanted was "the whole enchilada."[10] This referred mainly to the legalization of unauthorized Mexican immigrants in the United States and a large temporary worker program. Mexico had previously been quite diffident in pushing its position on migration issues. Mexico's migration policy before a change was made in the 1980s was to consciously have no policy in order to avoid interfering with U.S. policy in this area. The Mexican government learned that noninterference in U.S. policymaking was not normally reciprocated by the United States in Mexico. Migration issues are discussed in detail in chapter 6.

The second example reflecting Mexico's shift to assertiveness concerns the country's antinarcotics policy. President Felipe Calderón berated the United States for not contributing its fair share to a cooperative effort when he met with President George W. Bush in Mérida, Yucatán, in March 2007. Bush subsequently sought legislation to provide equipment to help Mexico in its struggle against the country's drug cartels. When the legislation was being considered in the judiciary committee of the U.S. Senate, a number of conditions were attached, including the requirement that the U.S. Department of State would have to verify that the Mexican police and military were not violating the human rights of those being accused of drug trafficking. It is important to keep in mind that thousands of Mexicans were being killed each year in a struggle among drug cartels for dominance in the lucrative U.S. drug market. The Mexican minister of Gobernación (usually translated as "minister of the interior"), Juan Camelo Mouriño, said on June 2, 2008, that these conditions were unacceptable because Mexico had a sovereign right to defend its national security and that human rights were well protected under Mexican law. In the end the legislation was worked out to the satisfaction of Mexico.[11] In large part this was accomplished after the use of quiet diplomacy by the Mexican ambassador in Washington, D.C.

Of these two examples of Mexico pushing its positions more aggressively than had been the norm, only the antinarcotics cooperation was successful. The second arena, on achieving the whole enchilada in the immigration field, did not succeed. The lesson from this partial record is evident: that an assertive policy stance will succeed or fail depending on the issue, the timing, the importance of the issue to the United States, and its context in the overall relationship.

Aspects of Negotiation

The dependency-dominance relationship can be observed over time in the way proposals are made and reacted to, but it also takes the form of not making any proposal at all. For example, Mexico did not make a proposal to negotiate bilateral trade with the United States until after the debt crisis in 1982 and the demise of its import-substitution policy. One purpose of this policy was to keep the United States at a distance. There really was nothing to negotiate as long as Mexico was unwilling to make import concessions and did not covet further expansion in the U.S. market. The logic of Mexico's export pessimism credo was that there was little purpose in growing Mexico's market in the United States, because this would lead to new U.S. import restrictions on the successful products.

Similarly, Mexico did not negotiate energy policy with the United States. Mexico, based on the letter of its constitution and the emotional antipathy to private equity investment in oil resources, had no basis on which to enter into joint ventures to find the funds and develop expertise for deepwater exploration for oil. For many years Mexico chose to have no stated migration policy relative to the United States, a position rationalized under the strongly held Mexican belief of no interference in the internal affairs of other countries. This policy of having no policy changed after the United States enacted immigration legislation of 1986, however, which for the first time limited the number of Mexican immigrants. After that the positions of the two countries reversed. It was the United States that refused to discuss general immigration issues—that is, other than migration of business and professional people, in the negotiations leading to the North American Free Trade Agreement (NAFTA). Indeed, the United States was blunt on this point: there would be no negotiation of U.S. general immigration policy if Mexico wanted negotiations on NAFTA to continue. The U.S. government at that time (1993) took the position that increased Mexican exports would lead to a decline in emigration to the United States. As was quickly learned, exactly the reverse happened.

Mexico's long history of diffidence in negotiating with the United States showed up in the concern about entering into NAFTA with the United States, even though it was the Mexican president, Carlos Salinas de Gortari, who had made the initial proposal. The fear of the Mexicans who were hesitant about NAFTA was that it was a high-risk adventure because Mexico would reluctantly have to adopt policies forcefully promoted by the United States.[12] Participants on the Mexican side of the NAFTA negotiation reported that U.S. negotiators were indeed tough, but that the chief negotiator, Julius (Jules) Katz, was true to his word: when he promised something, it was delivered. Indeed, the outcome of the negotiation was more balanced than a good many Mexican skeptics feared. A well-researched analysis of the negotiations by Antonio Ortiz Mena, a Mexican academic, argued that at the end of the day, Mexico achieved its main objective of improved access to the U.S. market for its goods and was able to maintain its position of making no important changes in energy policy—although one might question that keeping the status quo in energy best served Mexico's long-term interest.[13]

The literature on asymmetrical bargaining makes clear that the more powerful partner in a negotiation does not always prevail. John Odell, in a study written almost thirty years ago, noted that in twenty-five cases of dispute settlement involving the United States and Latin American countries, the outcome ended favorably for the United States in twelve cases, six ended in compromise, and the other seven ended favorably for the Latin American country.[14] William Habeeb, a consultant with expertise in international negotiation, has made the point that the weaker state generally has more at stake and will devote more energy to the issue, thereby altering the negotiating balance.[15] William Zartman, an expert on conflict management, in his analysis of why the weaker party gets traction in negotiations with stronger parties, makes particular reference to clever tactics, the distraction of the powerful country from many other issues, and the constraining effect on the powerful country of the entire relationship.[16]

Zartman's injunction to keep the entire relationship in mind is important. The United States would have preferred that Mexico loosen its restrictions on private equity investment in Mexican oil production and exploration, but it held back on this issue lest the entire negotiation collapse because of the intense opposition of the Mexican public to this change. No matter how much the United States wanted the change, no Mexican government up to this point in time has felt that it could propose the necessary constitutional amendment and survive. Mexico was able to say "no" because the entire relationship was at stake and the U.S. negotiators recognized this. Still, on issues important to the United States, its position will generally prevail. The U.S. position has prevailed on border security, on immigration, and on drug trafficking, although these positions may not be optimal, just as the Mexican position on oil may not be wise in the long run. These issues, in the U.S. scheme of things, are more important than the outcome of a single trade dispute in which the stakes tend to be relatively low.

The Mexico-U.S. Relationship in Context

Although the Mexico-U.S. relationship is evidently one between unequals, a reality that cannot be changed in the foreseeable future, it has also been influenced during the post-NAFTA period by the low economic growth of Mexico, lower indeed than that of the more developed United States over much of this period. The effect of the dependency-dominance dyad depends not just on the established relative power positions, but also on significant changes that are taking place. If Mexico had grown at, say, 7 percent a year since NAFTA instead of by 2 to 3 percent, its influence and bargaining position with the United States would be much stronger than it is today. Seven percent annual growth sustained over several decades is not fanciful—such countries as China and India have surpassed this.

Mexico's Growth Problem

The question to ask, consequently, is, Why has Mexican GDP growth been so low over this period? Given that Mexican exports have more than quadrupled from 1993, the year before NAFTA came into effect, to 2007, why didn't this raise GDP growth more? One partial answer is that imports grew almost as much, thereby limiting the increase in *net* exports; imports grew by about four times over this same period. However, Mexico's GDP growth since the economic crisis of 1982 through 2008 has been less than 2.5 percent a year, or about 0.5 percent per capita a year. During what has been dubbed the "Mexican miracle" (the period between 1961 and 1980), annual GDP growth was more than 6.5 percent a year, or about 3.5 percent per capita.[17] The 1980s are known in Latin America as the "lost decade," a decade of repetitive debt rescheduling and GDP growth of about 1 percent a year. The basic explanation for Mexico's low GDP growth after the miracle years has been the inability to make the structural changes that are essential for economic growth. Structural in this context includes such aspects of a country's socioeconomic underpinning as education, the justice system, labor laws and practices, the fiscal situation, the ability (or inability) to collect taxes, management of the energy sector, the extent of poverty, and the degree of income inequality among the population. These are the areas in which Mexico failed; or one can say, these are the areas in which the Mexican political system failed to promote the national interest and instead gave more attention to partisan politics and powerful special interests.

The bulk of the increased Mexican exports stimulated by NAFTA came from central Mexico, especially Mexico City and the neighboring state of Mexico, plus the six northern states that abut the United States, where most of the maquiladoras, or assembly plants, are located. The word "assembly" connotes a low level of value added; this was largely true when the maquiladora operations were created in the late 1960s to provide employment for the Mexicans who were expected to return home when the bracero program with the United States was ended in 1964. However, these facilities, where laborers add the labor-intensive aspects to partially completed products sent from the United States, have since become more sophisticated. The maquiladoras now produce auto and computer parts rather than the clothing and textile products that dominated maquiladora production in the early years.

The advantage of maquiladora production was that the tariff paid on the return of finished goods to the United States was only on the value added in Mexico. Once NAFTA came into existence, though, most U.S. import duties on goods originating in Mexico went to zero. Income and opportunity inequality among the Mexican states has long been a problem, and NAFTA widened the division. As an *Economist* special report on Mexico in the November 18–24, 2006, issue has indicated, nine states in south and southeast Mexico, which have about a quarter of the country's population, suffer from poor education and receive less investment than the more fortunate states in

central and northern Mexico.[18] This regional inequality is a structural problem and the relatively low level of economic growth in the poorer states limited the extent of national GDP growth occasioned by NAFTA.

Figure 1.1 shows the trajectory of real GDP growth (and declines) in
Mexico from 1954 through 2007. The year 1954 is chosen as the starting
date because there was a currency devaluation, and the new exchange rate
held steady for more than twenty years. The stability of the Mexican peso,
combined with a cautious development policy known as "stabilizing development," produced excellent results. The big shift to what was called "shared
development," ostensibly to reduce income inequality, took place during the
administration of Luis Echeverría Alvarez from 1970 to 1976. One of the outcomes of his *sexenio*, or six-year term, was the unsustainable inflation that
stemmed from large fiscal deficits that brought on currency devaluation at
the end of his term. This was the first of what became a succession of mostly
end-of-term sexenio crises that was not broken until the end of the term of
Ernesto Zedillo Ponce de León, when he passed the presidency to Vicente

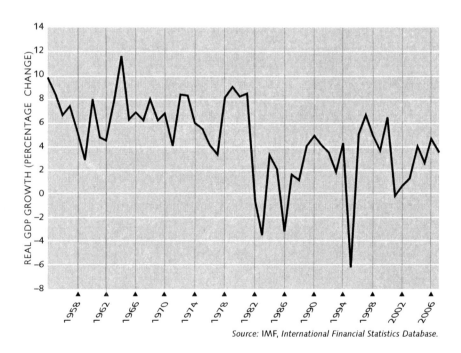

Source: IMF, *International Financial Statistics Database.*

Fig. 1.1. Mexico: Real GDP growth (percentage change), 1954–2007

Fox in 2000 without a currency crisis. These successive crises had a large impact on young people growing up in that period of some twenty-five years. They had learned that any pesos they had at the end of a sexenio would be worth less when the next sexenio began because of the expected devaluation. What they fathomed, if they were even slightly perceptive, was that it would be smart to get rid of pesos as best they could before the sexenio ended.

When Felipe Calderón Hinojosa delivered his first Informe, or message to the nation, on September 2, 2007, he noted that he inherited a stable economy, presumably to provide a contrast to the history of sexenio crises, and made the following points on economic deficiencies: insufficient economic growth, inadequate job-creation, insufficient infrastructure, need to collect more taxes to invest in social services, 40 percent of the population living in poverty and fourteen million living in extreme poverty, shrinking energy reserves, unequal opportunities, inadequate access to education, and environmental degradation. The key problems Calderón cited were structural in nature. Fox had done little to correct these inadequacies, and Calderón said he would tackle them. He faced a formidable problem in that while his party, the Partido Acción Nacional (PAN, the National Action Party), had a plurality of the seats in the chamber of deputies, it did not have a majority. This required that Calderón bargain with other parties, especially the PRI, to pass legislation to deal with structural impediments to economic growth.[19]

A word or two on the nature of the key economic structural issues is in order. A good place to start is the fiscal situation. Fiscal policy is part of any country's general economic policy and not necessarily structural in the sense defined earlier. The issue here is not one of equilibrium in revenue and expenditures, which has been achieved in Mexico in recent years, but rather how the revenue is raised, what programs are neglected, and the impact of these processes on other issues. Mexico, until the 2009 economic crisis, collected about 11 percent of GDP in taxes, which is low even by Latin American standards, and its expenditures are closer to 19 percent of GDP.[20] (For 2009, a year of economic crisis in Mexico, tax collections, according to the Bank of Mexico's central bank, was about 9 percent of the GDP.) Most of the difference, about 6 percent of GDP in normal years, is taken from the gross revenue of Petróleos Mexicanos (Pemex), the national oil company, to finance the general federal budget. Pemex has a monopoly on both upstream (exploration and production) and downstream (marketing, such as gasoline and diesel stations) oil operations. (Pemex also controls most natural gas exploration and production, but two other government-owned monopolies control electricity distribution, Comisión Federal de Electricidad and Luz y Fuerza del Centro. They are not efficient companies.) Consequently, Pemex in most years operates at a bookkeeping loss because of the large government take and is unable to finance its own exploration and production.[21]

Thus Pemex became a cash cow for funding the federal budget, rather than being able to operate in a businesslike manner. The company, the largest in Mexico, has been unsuccessful in recent years in finding enough new oil to replace the oil that is produced—and even that is declining rapidly, as old wells become less productive. Mexico's proven reserves are now down to an estimated nine years. The best prospects for finding new oil are in the deep waters of the Gulf of Mexico, and Pemex has no experience with such drilling and lacks the money to undertake take these expensive risks. Mexico has tried to entice foreign oil companies (both private and national) to drill in the deep waters of the Gulf under service contracts but has attracted little interest. These companies do not wish to act as service providers, but rather as equity risk takers able to book the oil as they seek financing and share in the benefits of success. Pemex is unable to do this because the Mexican constitution prohibits private equity in Mexico's oil resources.

The structural issue in the energy field is thus the combination of inadequate tax collection and the misuse of Pemex revenues, which has become a creature of the needs of Mexico's treasury ministry (the Secretaría de Hacienda y Credito Público). Consequently, neither tax collection nor the operation of Pemex is satisfactory. The Calderón administration was able, with the cooperation of the PRI, to convince the legislature to pass a new asset-based single-rate business tax in 2007 called the Impuesto Empresarial a Tasa Unica (IETU). Companies will pay the greater of either the new IETU or the existing income tax at 28 percent. The single rate started at 16.5 percent in 2008, rose to 17 percent in 2009, and reaches its final level of 17.5 percent in 2010. Without getting into the details of what is included in or excluded from the asset base on which this tax is calculated, it was expected to add as much as two additional percentage points of GDP to the government tax take. However, there is much business opposition to this tax, and it is unclear whether it will survive. A thoroughgoing tax overall is what is needed.

Mexico may become an oil importer by the end of the current sexenio or the beginning of the next if some corrective action is not taken. Pemex is unlikely to find another important oil deposit in the shallow waters of the Gulf of Mexico, as it did with Cantarell, one of the largest oil wells in the world and Mexico's largest single oil source. Mexico is already an importer of natural gas. Calderón succeeded in 2008 in getting new energy legislation enacted that focuses on making Pemex a stronger company, but it did not propose any constitutional change to allow private investment in Mexican oil operations.

Mexico has two groups of full-time workers: a first group, the formal workers, receives the benefits of the social security system, which include health care and retirement benefits, plus payments from employers if workers are discharged; and a second group, the "informal" (though legal) workers, who do not receive these benefits (although they do receive some social services from the government). The formal workers pay income taxes; the informal workers do not. The termination benefits to formal workers are typically three months of salary plus salary of twenty days per year of service. These immovability benefits, as they are called, were enacted at the urging of workers and labor unions to protect them in their dealings with their more powerful employers. However, employers have ways to avoid paying termination benefits by not hiring workers on a full-time basis, or by hiring them informally. About half of the workers in Mexico are formal and the other half informal. Many people in the informal economy are self-employed. The data on formal workers come from the social security institutions where they are registered.

The International Monetary Fund estimated that the size of the informal economy was 30 percent of GDP in 2006.[22] When the business tax mentioned earlier was enacted, another provision of the law was to impose a 2 percent tax on monthly cash bank deposits of more than twenty-five thousand pesos, as a way of getting people in the informal economy to pay their share. It is unclear if this will work as intended. Probably not, because there are many techniques for those targeted to avoid the tax, such as keeping monthly deposits less than twenty-five thousand pesos.

Mexico does not outdo all other countries in the number and significance of monopolies or oligopolies, but it is up there with the leaders. The key government institutions in Mexico dealing with oil, natural gas, and electricity distribution are monopolies. When Teléfonos de México (Telmex) was privatized in 1990, there was provision for a temporary six-year monopoly, but the private company was able to maintain monopoly prices for some eighteen years, although there are now stirrings of competition. Telmex has been one of the world's most expensive companies for long-distance telephone calls, as it added its local charges for transfers to and from overseas companies. Government officials, through the Fox administration, were complicit in allowing monopoly prices to continue. Calderón has shown greater concern over the adverse effects of monopolies. Telmex was the outstanding private example of Mexico's widespread oligopolies.

In addition to the cost of monopolies, special tax privileges for many companies are written into Mexico's budget. Tax avoidance and evasion are standard practice in Mexico, and there has been little will to crack down. The result is often higher prices in Mexico than in the United States, especially for such services such as the Internet, fixed and cellular telephones, residential and commercial electricity, cable television, and bank commissions on credit card purchases. During 2008 the price of gasoline was lower in Mexico than in the United States because of a government subsidy. This attracted U.S. drivers at the border to fill up their tanks in Mexico. The Asociación Nacional de Empresarios Independientes (ANEI), a lobbying organization of small and medium-sized businesses established to provide advice to Calderón, has argued that because the Mexican economy was opened to foreign competition after 1982, while the domestic economy remained replete with monopoly and oligopoly pricing, the competitive position of its member firms was compromised.[23]

Social Inequality

The most important structural problem in Mexico is primary and secondary education because its inadequacy compromises everything else well into the future. The Organization for Economic Cooperation and Development (OECD) reported that in 2003 money spent on education per student was higher in Mexico than the OECD average but that student performance in reading, math, and science was below the average. The implication is that much money was being misspent. Mexico spends about 25 percent of its education funds at the tertiary college and university level, and the rest at the primary and secondary levels combined. This is a form of subsidization of the rich; the cost to the student at the National University (Universidad Nacional Autónoma de México, UNAM) and to the public state universities is negligible. The labor union for primary and secondary education, the Sindicato Nacional de Trabajadores de Educación (SNTE), is one of Mexico's largest, with almost 1.5 million members, and most powerful *sindicatos*. It has been headed for years by Elba Esther Gordillo. She also has held high positions in the PRI, and there was even speculation that she was a *presidenciable*, a possible candidate for president of Mexico. She was not chosen and then left the PRI. The union has more power over disbursement of funds budgeted for primary and secondary education than does the government; it also dominates the hiring and replacement of teachers.

The comparison of expenditures and results between Mexico and other OECD countries is not fully fair. The OECD is a club of mainly rich countries (Mexico became a member in 1994), and the comparison with countries like those in Western Europe, Japan, Canada, and the United States will inevitably be unfavorable to Mexico. The first language for many in Mexico's Indian population is not Spanish, the country's poverty rates are higher than in the other OECD countries, and large areas of the countryside are isolated from population centers. There, some schools have no teachers, only teacher aides who oversee the children and turn recorded lessons on and off. Mexico will not attain its development goals unless its educational system is improved by bringing teachers to rural areas, providing students with books and equipment such as computers needed for a modern education, and truly delivering a program that leaves many fewer young persons behind.

Although its relations with the United States are deeper than those of any other country—except perhaps Canada—this is not showing up in the number of Mexicans studying in U.S. universities. More than 80 percent of Mexico's exports are to the United States, and most of the foreign investment in Mexico comes from the United States. For the 2006–2007 academic year, however, the Institute of International Education reported that Mexico ranked seventh among foreign countries sending students to tertiary-level education in the United States, behind India, China, South Korea, Japan, Taiwan, and Canada, respectively. Some of these countries are more populous than Mexico and some less populous. The number of Mexican students at the tertiary level in the United States in 2006–2007 was 13,826, or 2.4 percent of all foreign students. Some 60 percent of the Mexicans were undergraduates, unlike the students of other countries, where the focus is on specialized postgraduate studies in areas important to national development. Many of the Mexican students arrive with poor English skills. There is also a reverse flow of American students to Mexico, about ten thousand in 2005–2006, more than to any other Latin American country.[24]

Many Mexican students who study abroad, especially at the postgraduate level, are financed by scholarships from governments or other institutions. An organization named Comexus was created in 1990 to administer U.S. and

Mexican scholarly programs (the U.S. Fulbright Program and Mexico's García Robles Program). One way to expand graduate student interchange is to provide more funding to Comexus on both sides. Educational exchange is an important way to improve cultural and social interchange and for Mexicans to obtain the high-level technical education that is available in U.S. universities.

Visitors to Mexico see the beggars on the streets of Mexico's large cities and in popular tourist centers. When their taxis stop, they also observe the shows of juggling, acrobatics, fire eating, and the like of poor but energetic Mexicans seeking a handout of a few pesos. The visitors understand quickly that there is poverty in Mexico. The reality, however, is that they may be observing people who came to the cities from rural areas to escape even greater poverty. Mexico's worst poverty is in the rural areas that visitors rarely see. This rural poverty is systemic and hard to eliminate.[25]

Mexico's imports from the United States increased by 240 percent between 1994 and 2003—that is, after NAFTA came into effect—as compared with the average annual level of imports between 1984 and 1993. Simultaneously, Mexican corn production increased after 1994.[26] Corn is a staple food in Mexico. Much corn is produced by subsistence farmers in rain-fed areas (without irrigation) in southern and eastern states, where soil conditions are poor and where poverty has long existed. Some of the residents own small farms; others are sharecroppers and hired help who seek work on and around these farms at planting and harvest times. What many people from these areas do if they are even modestly risk-taking is to move to cities to improve their own lot and that of their families. The exit is not a tragedy, but the result of a normal desire to find something better. Trying to keep people in the rural areas may simplify the problems of cities but at the cost of much personal stagnation. In any case it is ineffective, and thus there is heavy migration from Mexico's poorest areas to the cities and thence across the border into the United States.

The situation for the very poorest has been improved in recent years by Mexico's groundbreaking and highly successful welfare program initially created under the name Progresa, now called Oportunidades. Providing food, education, and health support, Oportunidades is a palliative, original in its approach and now copied elsewhere, but it is not a solution.[27] Help also comes from remittances sent by migrants who cross the border into the United States without documents. For the people involved, a longer-term solution usually requires getting somewhere else. When the Mexican negotiators agreed, when

NAFTA was negotiated, to the duty-free entry of corn from the United States after fifteen years, the expectation was that the interval was long enough for job creation in the cities where the rural migrants were expected to go. The Mexican experts estimated wrong, however; Mexico's economic growth was not high enough after NAFTA went into effect.

Even though Mexico has had some success over the past decade in reducing poverty, a significant reduction requires high growth sustained year after year. The case most often cited in Latin America is Chile, where the number of people living in poverty was reduced from 41 percent in 1987 to 17 percent in 1994. This sharp, rapid decline was attributed to economic growth. Mexico has been unable to reduce its level of poverty to this extent because of the lack of sufficient, sustained GDP growth for some twenty-five years. Income inequality runs on its own track, one that is not parallel to poverty. For example, even as Chile's level of poverty declined sharply after 1986, its inequality rose. The Gini index, named after the Italian statistician Corrado Gini, is the technique generally used to show the extent of inequality and permits making comparisons across countries. The Gini coefficient is obtained by measuring the deviation between income percentiles and the income received by these percentiles of the population; the difference is the Gini coefficient. The higher it is, the more unequal the society is in income terms. If the population percentiles and the income each received were identical, the Gini index would be zero. Mexico's index is high, but according to the International Monetary Fund, it is lower than in Argentina, Brazil, and Chile.[28]

In the OECD's *Latin American Economic Outlook 2008*, one of the issues examined is "fiscal legitimacy"—namely, the degree of confidence people have in the government's performance in collecting and spending tax revenue. The proportion of the population in Mexico in 2005 that trusted that taxes were well spent was a mere 15 percent. The study also examined how taxes affect the Gini coefficient. According to the report, the Gini coefficient in Europe was 46 before taxes and 31 after taxes. In Mexico it was 51 before taxes, but still 49 after taxes—that is, not much improvement.[29] (This 2008 publication was the first edition of *Latin American Outlook*, which probably has something to do with the fact that the secretary-general of the OECD is a Mexican named Angel Gurría. He assumed this post on June 1, 2006; prior to that, he had been Mexico's foreign minister and then treasury minister.)

An important impediment to economic growth and political legitimacy in Mexico has been the lack of equal justice under the law. This affects investors who are not confident that they will get a fair hearing if brought before a court of law. Individuals in Mexico keep their distance from police, magistrates, and judges. If robbed, police are not generally informed by the victims for fear that a second robbery will take place. It is not uncommon for police to stop people in cars on highways with a trumped-up charge, seeking a bribe and implying that the alternative is arrest; it is common for victims not to report this to the authorities because the bribe-seekers have impunity.

President Calderón addressed the justice issue in his campaign and then followed up with a yearlong public discussion on the subject between the government, congress, academics, and nongovernmental organizations. On March 6, 2008, the Mexican congress approved an amendment to the constitution to strengthen the judicial system. It included provisions to institute an adversarial system based on trials (although this will take eight years to fully implement) and the presumption of innocence until proven guilty. Evidence obtained through methods that violate human rights will be suppressed, a guarantee of legal representation is included, and a new national public safety system will be set up to coordinate the work of the various entities in the fight against crime. The constitutional amendment process in Mexico requires the approval of sixteen of the thirty-one states.[30] The amendment looks promising on paper, but it will take time to evaluate its effectiveness.

Governance in Mexico

Mexico's transition in 2000 was remarkably smooth from what Mario Vargas Llosa, the Peruvian novelist and onetime political aspirant, has called a "perfect dictatorship" to what is today a democratic country. The change took place without violence. There were step-by-step concessions by successive administrations, a sort of setting the stage for the final action. Vicente Fox of the PAN was elected and routinely sworn in as president, thus ending the seventy-one-year presidential rule of the PRI, although not necessarily forever because the PRI may return to the top as the most competitive party. However, the alternation in power is no longer contested. That which had been barely possible now exists.

Effective democratic governance is not easy, and Mexico has little practice at it. The complexity of democracy, Mexican style, became manifest after 1997, when the PRI lost its majority in the lower house of the congress, possibly as a reaction to the country's deep depression in 1995. This was a watershed event in Mexico. The PRI president at the time, Ernesto Zedillo, was faced with the reality that he had to bargain with the legislature to get his initiatives enacted into law. This was new in modern Mexico. Bargaining did not work well, in part because the two main opposition parties, then the PAN and the PRD (Partido de la Revolución Democrática, the Party of the Democratic Revolution) were intent on furthering their own interests, and in part because each party had to cater to powerful special interests that were important to it.

This is still the case. Vicente Fox, on the one hand, had practically no success in dealing with the legislature, where the opposition was the PRI and the PRD. Felipe Calderón, on the other hand, has shown that he is willing to bargain with the congress, and he had some successes in his first year in office. He had more difficulty in his second year as president, however.[31] The PRD is the party of Andrés Manuel López Obrador, who narrowly lost the presidency to Calderón in 2006, and the party is not inclined to bargain with Calderón on such issues as altering the structure of the energy sector, an important initiative in 2008. As one examines the inability of the authoritarian PRI presidents to obtain the structural changes needed for higher economic growth, even when the legislature was a rubber stamp, it is not surprising that this is even more difficult when power is divided between the executive and legislative branches. Mexico is a prime example of the way that special interest and rent-seeking groups retard national economic growth, famously analyzed in the United States by the best-known academic analyst on this subject, Mancur Olson.[32]

A November 18, 2006, survey of Mexico in the *Economist* concluded that the old political model had died and a new one had yet to be born. The many decades of strong presidents had turned into a time of weak presidents. A redundant congress had turned into a quarrelsome one. State governors had little national influence under the old system and were now important, perhaps in compensation for the weaker presidents. It might help if deputies and senators were allowed to run for reelection, perhaps for one more term for senators and two more terms for deputies (allowing both senators and deputies to hold office for a total of twelve years) to make them less dependent on their parties for their next jobs. However, even if this were to happen, it might not work out that way.

In the past Mexico has made major policy changes after crises. By about 1970 it was evident to Mexican economists that the postwar import-substitution policy had run its useful course, but the change to a more open economy did not occur until after the economic crisis of 1982. The fixed-rate exchange rate system showed deep strain throughout all of 1994, but the change to a more flexible system took place only after the peso crashed at the end of the year, leading to economic depression in 1995. Many Mexican experts think that energy policy may go through a similar pattern should Mexico be forced to import oil, just as it now imports natural gas. It is hard to know what should be done to make Mexican democracy more meaningful. The likely answer is to allow time for this to happen.

One final point to make about Mexican democracy is to question whether the country's politicians are as enthusiastic about democracy as outsiders would like them to be. Mexico had established a federal electoral system (Instituto Federal Electoral, the IFE) and a separate tribunal to monitor elections and electoral activities. The system was dominated by an independent president and members chosen because of their distinguished backgrounds, and this structure worked well over several elections. Indeed, the IFE structure was superior to the party-dominated electoral monitoring system in the United States. The IFE played a central role in handling complaints from the PRD and its presidential candidate, López Obrador, in 2006. However, after the election, at the insistence of the PRD and with the support of the PRI, Mexico chose to make its monitoring body more like that of the party-dominated U.S. structure. President Calderón consented to this to get the necessary votes to pass the tax legislation discussed earlier. Many leading Mexican intellectuals protested the idea of making the IFE subject to the very political parties competing for election, but to no avail. Mexico must collect more taxes, but it also needs a strong electoral system. Trading away the latter for the former may turn out to have been an unfortunate deal.

Problem-Solving Techniques

The rest of the book explores how the Mexican and the U.S. governments have approached each other (and still largely do) in their conduct of economic relations—the former as an overly defensive nation and the latter as one that is often excessively aggressive. These approaches have changed over time as the objective situation changes, but the vestiges of old habits are deeply embedded in their respective national characteristics. The premise from which this analysis unfolds is that these approaches are not optimal, and consequently often lead to suboptimal economic relations.

This does not imply that *all* economic interactions are of this defensive-aggressive nature. Mexico knows how to say "no" when an issue is important to it or is considered to be extremely sensitive, such as the refusal to negotiate any changes in oil policy in NAFTA. The Mexican authorities also know how to chip away at undesirable U.S. actions, especially when prodded by its private sector. Several examples of eventual solutions to trade disputes show this. The U.S. for many years imposed restrictions on Mexican avocados to prevent the transfer of pest infestation into the United States—restrictions that were legitimate in their time. The Mexicans worked on the problem and in the early 1990s convinced U.S. agricultural authorities to conduct joint annual surveys of pest incidence over four years. The surveys demonstrated that pest infestations were under control. But it took until 2007 to progressively open the U.S. market, because of the resistance of U.S. avocado producers to face fierce Mexican competition.

Another example is the long effort of U.S. tomato growers, especially from Florida, to prevent or limit the import of fresh Mexican tomatoes. This restrictive effort took various forms: U.S. Department of Agriculture marketing regulations demanding uniform size in any carton of fresh tomatoes; antidumping cases alleging that Mexican tomatoes were being sold at less than fair value in the United States; and agreements forced on Mexico for floor prices to limit price competition with U.S. tomatoes and also "voluntary" export restraints by Mexico.[33] Today, the market is largely open (and the Mexican tomatoes are largely vine-ripened).

Yet another example of an eventual solution to a trade dispute revolves around U.S. antidumping restrictions against cement exported to the United States by Cementos Mexicanos (Cemex). These restrictions were maintained for sixteen years, until 2006. Cemex is one of the largest cement producers in the world. In 2000 the firm actually bought the U.S. company that brought the original antidumping case. The restrictions were lifted because of cement shortages stemming from Hurricane Katrina in 2005, plus the supportive effort against the restrictions by the U.S. secretary of commerce.[34] In each case of these cases the Mexican authorities persisted, with the help of U.S. legal advice, and eventually prevailed. The Mexican private sector operating cooperatively with the Mexican government can be both persistent and patient when dealing with U.S. trade restrictions.

One question consistently comes up: Why doesn't Mexico simply ask for what it wants? The same question can be asked in reverse: Why doesn't the

United States always ask for what it wants? The reality is that there are some objectives that cannot be resolved by bilateral negotiations. The Mexican government should want the use of narcotics in the United States to be decriminalized as a way to curtail the enormous rents obtained by drug cartels precisely because they are peddling illegal products. Mexico, however, cannot formally make this suggestion; U.S. drug policy is made in the United States. The United States would like Mexico to maximize its oil exploration and production and, deep down, thinks this would best be achieved by permitting joint ventures between Pemex and foreign oil companies. But the U.S. government cannot say this because Mexico will make its own oil policy. Most Mexicans would be grateful for more aid from the United States along the lines used in the European Union to assist "backward" regions. Mexican authorities are reluctant to say this because they don't know the conditions the United States would put on its foreign aid (this is precisely what happened in the Mérida Initiative, which is detailed in chapter 4). Countries have to be careful what they ask for; they might get more than they asked for, as the United States learned from its programs seeking temporary immigrants.

Problems in specific areas cannot usually be resolved in isolation from the general context in each country. James Jones, who was the U.S. ambassador to Mexico from 1993 to 1997, has made the point that there are deep knowledge gaps in each country about the other—especially in the United States—and this complicates the resolution of problems.[35] The current context in the United States, as well as that in Mexico, will certainly change, and understanding these changes will be crucial to more informed policymaking on both sides of the border.

Trade
From Closure to Opening

A change in our attitude toward our hegemonic neighbor to the
north had to be fostered.
—CARLOS SALINAS DE GORTARI, 2000

A nation that would enrich itself by foreign trade is certainly
most likely to do so when its neighbors are all rich, industrious,
and commercial nations.
—ADAM SMITH, 1776

M exico, during the first ten years of the twentieth century, was preoccupied with the enormous violence of the Revolution of 1910,
and after that with the uncertainty of the country's political structure. The event that attracted most attention to Mexico in the 1930s was the
expropriation of foreign oil companies in 1938. During the great depression
of the 1930s, Latin American countries had to largely fend for themselves
because U.S. imports from them declined sharply, as did the prices of their
key commodities. Consequently, Latin American countries lacked the funds
to import what they needed. Mexico fared better than most during the early
stage of the depression, because its cash reserves were high in 1930, but these
were dissipated in 1931.[1] Hence, attention on formulating a comprehensive
trade policy was generally delayed until after World War II. By then, most
Latin American countries, including Mexico, were used to getting much of
what they needed in their home markets.

The Import-Substitution Years

After the war Raúl Prebisch, an Argentine economist, provided a reasoned rationale for continuing to buy most goods in domestic markets. Prebisch was the executive secretary of the Economic Commission for Latin America (the Comisión Económica para América Latina, CEPAL) from 1948 to 1962. His most influential book, *The Economic Development of Latin America and Its Principal Problems*, published in 1950, argued that there was a secular tendency for commodity prices to decline, particularly in agriculture, whereas the prices of manufactured products increased over time. Using an economic term, Prebisch was asserting that Latin America's "terms-of-trade" were likely to deteriorate further. Even though he included data from other periods, he was generalizing from the experience of the depression. Prebisch preached that the path to economic development in Latin America, or what he called the "periphery" of underdeveloped countries generally, was to industrialize and rid themselves of the influence of what he called the "center." This import-substitution prescription, also called import-substituting industrialization (ISI), was adopted throughout Latin America in the 1960s.

ISI was a variation of the infant industry argument of development that predated Prebisch's work and focused on the Latin American experience. Alexander Hamilton, who later became the first U.S. secretary of the treasury, published his *Report on Manufactures* in 1791 and it showed thinking similar to that of Prebisch more than a century later, although without the terms-of-trade foundation that Prebisch used. Hamilton's report became the ideology of the land, but in practice it made little headway in the United States, whereas Prebisch's ideas were widely adopted in Latin America. This center-periphery philosophy was further expanded in the 1960s into the dependency theory in Latin America. This theory argued that the developed "center" deliberately tried to keep the underdeveloped "periphery" from growing, so that the center could purchase cheap commodities produced by exploited labor.

Asian countries—Japan after the Meiji restoration, and Korea, Taiwan, Singapore, and others after World War II—adopted a different development paradigm: namely, to rely on export growth, rather than to adopt the "export pessimism" of Latin America. The Asian countries, however, generally did not open their markets to imports; instead, they used a combination of limiting imports and pushing exports. During the 1960s and into the 1970s, Latin America suffered from high inflation and consequently from periodic overvalued exchange rates. The tendency in Asia during this period was to keep exchange rates undervalued to deter imports and expand exports. China in recent years has adopted precisely this policy. India came later than China to export promotion and consequently came late to achieving high rates of GDP growth.

It is overstatement to say that Latin American ISI policy was a complete failure, however. There was considerable growth in many Latin American countries during the years of import substitution, including Mexico (as figure 1.1 shows), but on the whole Asia overtook Latin America. For example, South Korea's GDP in 1954 was $22.1 billion ($1,065 per capita) and was $705.6 billion in 2007 ($14,388 per capita), whereas the GDP data for Mexico during the same years was $62.8 billion in 1954 ($2,009 per capita) and $688.8 billion in 2007 ($6,465 per capita).[2] When Prebisch was asked why Latin America did not adopt the more dynamic East Asian policies, his standard answer was that the two regions were different.[3]

ISI policy suited Mexico in terms of its desired political relations with the United States. Mexico wanted to assert its nationalism that the United States had repeatedly dismissed for more than a century before Mexico turned its attention to post–World War II trade policy. The examples of the United States exhibiting its dominant demeanor are numerous, such as U.S. interference during the Mexican Revolution, its later military forays into Mexico, and its adamancy in the 1920s and 1930s that led Lázaro Cárdenas to expropriate the holdings of foreign oil companies. Mexico's standard foreign policy dictum of noninterference in the internal affairs of other countries was developed mainly as a criticism of the United States—although there had been other foreign interference in Mexico, such as the French intervention and the installation of Maximilian and Carlota as emperor and empress of Mexico in 1864 while the United States was engaged in its Civil War.

Mexico had no need for extensive trade negotiations with the United States because it was not prepared to open its market very much to imports or to actually negotiate improved access to the U.S. market.[4] Instead, Mexico was expanding the scope of its ISI policies. These policies began by focusing on Mexico's consumer products, then expanded to the intermediate products needed to produce consumer goods, and eventually ISI found its way into the production of capital goods. For the most part the ISI industries were not competitive, but they did stimulate employment in urban areas. Mexican producers had to buy specified proportions of their intermediate products locally, even if they were more expensive and inferior in quality to what could be imported. The system was destined to augment income inequality because the producers faced little competition, paid low wages, and set prices that could not be undercut by imports.

Efficiency was not a high priority because industrial producers were not generally encouraged to export their products. There was extensive use of import permits and quotas, and before the 1970s there was no good measurement of import protection. The first solid paper to provide empirical evidence of the levels of protection, nominal and effective, written by Gerardo M. Bueno, was published in 1972.[5] There was considerable sentiment among economists in Mexico by the early 1970s that import substitution had run its useful course. It was hard to change development policy at that time because the Mexican economy was growing reasonably well, and there were powerful entrenched interests who profited from keeping the policy in place. The timeline at the end of the chapter provides the dates of relevant U.S.-Mexico trade activities.

Post-1982: Change of Paradigm

The crash that put an end to ISI came in 1982, when Mexico was unable to service its foreign debt. The Mexican finance minister Jesús Silva-Herzog came to Washington, D.C., to speak with officials of the U.S Treasury and the International Monetary Fund, seeking to postpone debt payments. What followed were repeated debt reschedulings with Mexico and other Latin American countries. The issue was resolved only in 1989, when the U.S. treasury secretary Nicholas Brady proposed a scheme under which Mexico and other debtor countries could borrow dollar-denominated bonds backed by zero-coupon U.S. securities. The link between the 1982 economic crash and Mexico's ISI policy was not unique, but it nevertheless provided the stimulus to change a trade policy already considered outdated by most Mexican economists.

The elements that led to the 1982 crash were a mixture of just about all of Mexico's development policies. One element was the energy program. Mexico was able to exploit large oil finds that came on stream during the administration of President José López Portillo (1976–1982), and oil exports quickly took precedence over all other exports. In 1982 petroleum and mining exports amounted to 70 percent of the total, manufactures only 25 percent, agricultural products 5 percent.[6] López Portillo seemed to think that oil prices would remain consistently high and that would give Mexico much leverage in its relations with the United States. Instead of staying high, however, oil prices fell in 1981 amid what was then referred to as an oil glut. The second element was the reality of low exports of other things, a consequence of the Mexican policy of keeping its distance from the U.S. market.

A third element was a sharp change in the interest rates Mexico had to pay for its borrowings in the U.S. market. U.S. inflation was high when in 1979, Paul Volcker was named chairman of the Federal Reserve Board by President Jimmy Carter. Volcker led the Fed in drastic anti-inflation measures. In May 1981 the average return on ninety-day treasury bills was 16.2 percent. Annual U.S. inflation was brought down from 11–12 percent to 4–5 percent by September 1982. Much of Mexico's earlier borrowings had been at rates that were effectively negative because of the inflated dollars with which they were repaid, whereas repayments by 1982 became positive.

The fourth and final relevant element of Mexican policy was its wariness about receiving foreign direct investment. Alongside ISI in trade, Mexico was concerned about U.S. control of Mexican industries leading to control over key aspects of the national economy; this was coupled with what was seen as the high cost to Mexico when dividends of U.S. and other foreign investors were sent to the home country. Mexico, consequently, chose to rely more heavily on foreign debt financing of industries rather than foreign equity ownership—this was seen as limiting U.S. dominance and being cheaper, given the interest rate experience in the late 1970s. Mexico learned in the 1982 debt crisis that foreign debt financing had a significant downside.

Mexican GDP growth remained sluggish throughout the 1980s; per capita GDP fell by an average of half of 1 percent a year during that decade. This was accompanied by substantial growth in the informal economy. The economist Gustavo Vega Cánovas has pointed out that it took nine years after the 1982 crisis to recover precrisis levels of industrial production.[7] By contrast, it took just one year to recover levels of industrial production after the severe 1994–1995 economic crisis. One difference was that the latter crisis grew out of an exchange rate problem, whereas in 1982 the causes of the crisis were systemic. As a result of the trade policy changes instituted after 1982, Mexico's oil exports came down to 30 percent of the total export value in 1989, and the value of manufactured goods exports that year rose to about 60 percent.[8] By 2005 oil and mining exports as a percentage of total export value fell to less than 15 percent, and manufacturing exports rose to more than 81 percent of the total.[9] The change in commercial policy is what Vega focused on in his work on the commercial opening of the Mexican economy after 1982.

A process of accumulating changes in development policy took place after 1982, first cautiously under President Miguel de la Madrid, then more radically under Carlos Salinas de Gortari (1988–1994), and consolidated under Ernesto Zedillo (1994–2000). Mexico in this period joined GATT, reduced import tariffs, rescinded import permits, abandoned the official (arbitrary) price valuation for imports, and concluded the NAFTA agreement with the United States and Canada. Mexico also concluded other free trade agreements (FTAs) during this period. Complementary measures were taken in other areas, particularly putting out a welcome mat to attract foreign direct investment. Although many tariffs were reduced unilaterally, negotiation was at the heart of the new trade policy. In the case of foreign direct investment, where negotiation between the Mexican government and investors had been the norm, an ideal situation for bribery, the shift was the reverse of trade— largely to automaticity.

The opening of the Mexican economy after 1982 was chiefly directed by Mexican economists who had obtained advanced degrees from many of the most prestigious U.S. universities. Mexico changed from minimizing economic and political relations with the United States to greater openness stimulated by philosophic contagion from training by U.S. academics. These steps, taken successively, discarded the policy that had existed for decades under which Mexico consciously sought to keep the United States at a distance. The Mexican academic Macario Schettino has dated the changes from 1986, when the economic policy that he refers to as "neoliberalism" began to be imposed, as opposed to the "pre-modern" regime that had prevailed since the presidency of Lázaro Cárdenas and the oil expropriation of 1938. He argues that the Mexican regime that existed for most of the twentieth century was authoritarian and antiliberal, shunned competency, and was self-admiring and stubborn about receiving foreign ideas.[10]

NAFTA Alters Trade and Investment Relations

President Salinas has written that he realized that the foreign direct investment Mexico needed to increase GDP growth would not come from Western Europe because of its preoccupation with Eastern Europe after the

Berlin Wall came down.[11] He then turned to the United States. Salinas's first idea was to conclude a series of sector agreements with the United States, but this generated little traction because each country wanted to negotiate in those sectors in which it was most competitive.[12] He then approached the U.S. president George H. W. Bush in June 1990 about the possibility of a bilateral FTA. Bush was interested. John Negroponte, then U.S. ambassador to Mexico, was present at the meeting.[13] He noted that a number of Texans who saw benefits to the United States of higher Mexican economic growth favored the idea of an FTA and were close to Bush 41. (George H. W. Bush was the forty-first president of the United States.) These men included James Baker, then secretary of state, and Robert A. Mossbacher, then secretary of commerce. Negroponte's point was that with respect to an FTA with the United States, Mexico had friends in high places. But the most senior officials of the Office of the U.S. Trade Representative (USTR), those who would be responsible for negotiating the FTA, preferred to delay the trade talks with Mexico until after the Uruguay Round of trade negotiations underway in Geneva, in GATT, were completed. USTR was overruled, however, and in the end it turned out that NAFTA was useful in stimulating the successful conclusion of the Uruguay Round because it included issues still in dispute in Geneva on investment, intellectual property, and government procurement.

Once it was clear that the United States and Mexico were going ahead with trade negotiations, the Canadian government said it wished to join the talks as well. Canada and the United States had already agreed to an FTA that had gone into effect on January 1, 1989.[14] The Canadian rationale was to avoid having what it called a hub-and-spoke arrangement under which the United States would have free trade with both Mexico and Canada (the United States would be the hub), and each of them would have free trade only with the United States (Canada and Mexico would be the spokes). There was some suspicion in USTR that the Canadians might be entering the NAFTA negotiations to be a spoiler, to avoid sharing their trade preferences in the U.S. market with Mexico. An informal warning was given to Canadian negotiators that if they seemed to be preventing progress, they would be excluded from the negotiations.

People approaching NAFTA anew some fifteen years after the agreement came into effect must make an effort to understand how unlikely such an agreement would have been in, say, the 1970s. Few political analysts of the Mexico-U.S. relationship at that time would have considered such an agreement realistic, then or subsequently. Even after the events of 1982, the idea of free trade in most products between the two countries was largely unthinkable for political reasons.[15] Salinas realized this, and his management of turning around Mexican opinion was masterful. He probably could not have achieved the turnaround in Mexican public opinion that he did had he not been an authoritarian leader. When the agreement was vetted for approval in the Mexican legislature, Salinas controlled the debate in the Senate, largely bypassing the Chamber of Deputies, where there were more opposition deputies. The public relations machinery of Los Pinos, the presidential residence, went into full gear about the benefits for Mexico of access to the U.S. market. Salinas overpromised, saying that economic growth would be higher and that migration from Mexico would be substantially replaced by goods produced at home by Mexican workers. The U.S. government oversold the benefits of NAFTA as well, but in the end the agreement barely made it through the U.S. House of Representatives. The assertions regarding an upswing in Mexican GDP and a downsizing of migration to the United States turned out to be wrong on both counts.

The actual negotiations surrounding the agreement were rigorous. Each of the three negotiating countries refused to give concessions on issues they considered important to them: Mexico on energy and finance; the United States on immigration and cabotage; and Canada on cultural issues and agriculture.[16] The United States made concessions on sugar in the agreement, but then retracted them.[17] The United States agreed in NAFTA that unrestricted trucking of goods would be permitted six years after NAFTA went into effect—that is, in year 2000—but the United States has refused to implement this provision, allegedly on safety grounds. All countries have special interests.

When Bill Clinton assumed the U.S. presidency in 1993, it became clear that the votes to approve the enabling legislation to put NAFTA into effect were not there. The principal opposition came from Democrats in the House who had aligned themselves with the organized U.S. labor movement that vehemently opposed NAFTA. Organized labor was opposed because of concern over competition with a country whose labor costs were much lower; Mexican labor costs in manufacturing were about 15 percent of those of workers in manufacturing in the United States. There was also opposition from many environmental groups that were concerned about Mexico's environmental practices. To meet these problems, the United States was able to negotiate parallel agreements to NAFTA on these two issues. The environmental side agreement was more substantive than the labor accord, in large part because some environmental organizations cooperated in fashioning the agreement. President Clinton also obtained support from past presidents and past secretaries of state, was willing to negotiate the withdrawal of some concessions from the NAFTA agreement that already had been signed, and had made unrelated offers to get wavering congressmen to vote in favor of the agreement. After all these steps Clinton got barely enough votes to put the agreement into effect. The labor movement never fully forgave Clinton for his actions and has continued its opposition to NAFTA ever since.

The most complete contemporaneous analyses of NAFTA negotiations can be found in a series of books coauthored by Gary C. Hufbauer and Jeffrey J. Schott.[18] In the subsequent fifteen years, writing about NAFTA, pro and con and in between, became something of a cottage industry. The themes covered by these various writings include trade outcomes, the effects of the agreement on U.S. employment, how NAFTA affected the broad Mexico-U.S. relationship, and what should be done about the future of NAFTA. Some opinions on many of these issues, particularly with respect to Mexico and the United States, follow.[19]

NAFTA, at its base, is an agreement designed to increase trade among the member countries and to encourage foreign direct investment into Mexico. Both these objectives were achieved. Mexican merchandise exports to the United States were about $43 billion in 1993, the year before NAFTA went into effect, and they were $223 billion in 2007, all in current dollars. Adjusting for inflation, Mexican exports quadrupled over this period. Mexican imports from the United States went from $45 billion in 1993 to $140 billion in 2007, both figures in current dollars; this was substantial but not as much of an increase as in the reverse direction.[20] Trade would have increased even without NAFTA, but econometric analysis does demonstrate that there was a positive NAFTA effect. Foreign direct investment in Mexico also rose sharply, from about $2.7 billion a year in the ten years before NAFTA came into effect to more than $15 billion a year during the ten years after NAFTA. Foreign direct investment into Mexico was $23.2 billion in 2007 but fell to $18.6 billion in 2008 as a result of the U.S. financial crisis in that year.[21] The Latin Americanist Carol Wise, using World Bank sources, has written that without NAFTA, Mexico's exports would have been 50 percent lower and foreign direct investment about 40 percent less than it was.[22]

After 2000 the increase in Mexican exports to the United States took place in the face of substantial competition from China. U.S. imports from China, primarily manufactured goods, increased by 187 percent between 2000 and 2006, while those from Mexico grew by only 46 percent.[23] In 2007, China was the second largest exporter of goods to the United States, after Canada, and Mexico was third. However, Mexico remained the second largest market for U.S. exports, after Canada, and China was fifth. Mexico is most competitive in the U.S. market as compared with China when goods have a high ratio of weight to value (such as motor vehicles, large screen televisions, and major household appliances), are high-quality manufactured goods (medical goods, process control instruments) rather than those with lower prices, and are inputs for just-in-time delivery (such as auto parts). In 2006 motor vehicles and parts accounted for 24 percent of Mexican exports to the United States.[24] It is unclear how this trade will develop as the U.S.-owned automobile industry is being restructured in 2009.

However, after fifteen years the trade benefits from NAFTA have tapered off. Nevertheless, there would be adverse trade and investment effects if the agreement were terminated. The structure of NAFTA plays a large role in North American trade because there is assurance of beneficial trade treatment. This assurance also encourages investment in Mexico. If NAFTA were terminated, it is not clear what would happen to the preferential trade treatment that exists under the agreement, whether free trade would continue in North America or return to the pre-NAFTA situation of 1993. Mexico has many other FTAs, the most important of which is with the European Union; if, without NAFTA, Mexican tariffs rise on imports from the United States, they would face discrimination as compared with EU exports to Mexico. If NAFTA were terminated, as was intimated as a possibility during the Democratic presidential primary campaign of 2008, another agreement would have to be negotiated to replace it.

Wise's article on NAFTA, "Unfulfilled Promise," explores the uneven pattern of economic convergence between Mexico and its NAFTA partners and within Mexico itself.[25] A similar argument was made in a 2003 report of the Carnegie Endowment for International Peace, "NAFTA's Promise and Reality," where the reasoning was that NAFTA did not help Mexico's economy keep pace with the growing demand for jobs.[26] Why blame NAFTA if it accomplished its primary objectives of stimulating Mexican exports and encouraging foreign direct investment into the country? There is no logic in the argument that Mexican GDP growth faltered *because* its exports increased—and this is what the "blame NAFTA" argument amounts to. There is a much better explanation for Mexico's low to nil economic growth over the past fifteen years: Mexico's failure to build on NAFTA's trade stimulus by undertaking the complementary structural reforms that are necessary to achieve growth.[27] Mexico's failure to meet economic expectations after 1994 was not because that year was the onset of NAFTA; rather, the failure was inaction on Mexico's structural inadequacies. The inability of the Mexican political system to make these structural adjustments remains a serious problem to date.

NAFTA was oversold in the negotiation and legislative approval stages by both the U.S. and Mexican governments. The agreement was not a panacea, something that by itself would raise Mexico's rate of economic growth and reduce unauthorized migration to the United States, but it was sold this way by both governments, especially by President Salinas of Mexico. The agreement was useful in the nontrade aspects of the Mexico-U.S. relationship. Most official interaction was initiated by the Mexican government before NAFTA took place via the state department, although there were regular contacts between the two treasury departments. There was little direct contact between the Mexican embassy in Washington, D.C., and members of the U.S. Congress. The Mexican embassy, before the NAFTA negotiating process, did little to monitor the progress of congressional action and how this might have sideswiped Mexican interests, something that the Canadian embassy in Washington did meticulously.

The Mexican government did little lobbying before NAFTA because it believed in noninterference in the internal affairs of other countries. Government officials in Mexico generally did not know their counterparts in departments other than in the state department, even though much of the action relevant to Mexico took place in such departments as agriculture, commerce, labor, and others. NAFTA changed all of this, and the pre-NAFTA pattern is history—quaint history of naïveté about how Washington works. Hermann von Bertrab, who coordinated Mexican efforts in Washington during the NAFTA negotiations, has recounted the contacts that Mexico made with members of the U.S. Congress during that process. He has also identified the legal and lobbying efforts that Mexico took in Washington.[28] It is now considered standard Mexican operating procedure to track activities in the U.S. Congress and to lobby in Washington and the United States in favor of its positions.

NAFTA brought about important nontrade changes in the Mexico-U.S. relationship. Mexican actions in Washington—such as making direct contact with members of congress, hiring Washington trade attorneys, carrying on direct conversations between Mexican and U.S. counterparts without the intervention of the state department—largely transformed the previous formal and distant relationship into one similar to that between Canada and the United States. The asymmetry between Mexico and the United States is greater than that between Canada and the United States, but behavioral patterns in the two relationships are converging. This leads to more equal interaction between Mexico and the United States in many substantive areas.[29]

Looking Ahead

The current discussion on the Mexico-U.S. trade relationship is about the direction it should take. Public opinion surveys in each country show considerable ambivalence about this. Many people believe that little should be done to strengthen NAFTA, and just as many believe the reverse. The terrorist destruction of the Twin Towers of the World Trade Center on September 11, 2001, led to an augmentation of security controls at the U.S. borders with Mexico and Canada, which affected trade and other issues. The phrase "security trumps trade" was heard frequently, but this was quickly replaced with what one Mexican analyst called "protection without protectionism."[30] The Security and Prosperity Partnership of North America (SPP) agreement, which occurred at a summit of the countries' three leaders in March 2005, has had little impact on the trajectory of NAFTA. The SPP became the target of conspiracy theorists in the United States who argued that its purpose was to clandestinely lay the foundation for a "North American Union" that was not really defined. Although the SPP process had some success—such as eliciting business recommendations on improving regional competitiveness through the North American Competitive Council—it is largely unknown to the populations of the three countries. Some explanations of why the SPP has had little constructive influence include opposition to NAFTA by many people in Canada, Mexico, and the United States; the exclusion of congress from the process; and the inherent difficulty of finding consensus among the three countries on what the next integrative steps should be.[31] The SPP was terminated in August 2009 when the leaders of the three NAFTA countries met in Guadalajara, Mexico.

Robert Pastor, a U.S. academic and onetime government policy official, has taken an expansive view of what must be done to accelerate the North American integration process. He has advocated the adoption of a customs union with a common external tariff to replace the existing FTA (under which each country maintains its own tariffs against imports from non-NAFTA countries). Pastor also believes in the creation of a community of North America and adopting many features that exist in the European Union, particularly financial help to less-developed regions.[32] A task force of the U.S. Council on Foreign Relations (CFR) published a report in 2005 entitled "Building a North American Community," which contained a number of recommendations on trade and other issues. The main trade-related suggestions were to adopt a common external tariff for North America, establish a seamless North American market for trade, help Mexico to intensify in economic development efforts, and adopt a North American approach to regulation.[33] Pastor was the vice chair of the CFR task force, and the report shows that he was influential in tailoring its recommendations. Jeffrey Schott, a trade expert, in his discussion of intra-NAFTA trade negotiations, has put much emphasis on the fact that Canada, Mexico, and the United States each have three-dimensional trade policies: bilateral, hemispheric, and multilateral. He states that a common external tariff would have benefits in that it could eliminate rules of origin to determine what goods are national and therefore eligible for free trade. But this view also has problems.[34]

Important statements about the future of NAFTA and of North American integration came from then presidential candidate Barack Obama during the Democratic Party primaries. During the primaries Obama said that NAFTA should be renegotiated to strengthen the labor and environmental provisions now contained in the two side agreements. He also said that the more stringent provisions should become an intrinsic part of NAFTA. The adamancy with which he espoused this position in the primary contest with candidate Hillary Clinton (who adopted much the same position) has since softened, and the renegotiate-NAFTA theme is either on the back burner or has been abandoned.

One is reminded of the Mexican position that was prevalent during 2006 and 2007 to renegotiate NAFTA's agricultural provisions to prevent the complete removal of tariffs on Mexican imports of corn, beans, and other products that were about to take place after the fifteen-year transition (the usual transition time was ten years or less) specified in the original agreement for sensitive products. Even Vicente Fox, Mexico's president before Felipe Calderón, supported renegotiation of NAFTA's agriculture provisions. The position was surreal, and the Mexicans backed away when reminded that if any part of NAFTA was reopened, this would open the entire agreement to changes the other member countries wanted—including some that Mexico might detest, such as limiting its considerable agricultural exports of fresh fruits and vegetables.

President Obama's position on labor and environment was equally surreal. One way around this is to renegotiate the two side agreements because this would not open NAFTA itself to other changes Mexico and Canada would like. Or a trilateral agreement could be reached on what a revised NAFTA would look like before opening formal negotiation. Any change in NAFTA presumably would require enabling legislation by the U.S. Congress, and it is not evident that President Obama, supported by a bigger Democratic majority in both houses, would get this approval. The Democrats almost surely would be too beholden to organized labor to vote in favor of changes, even if these strengthened the labor provisions. The organized labor position is to kill NAFTA, as it has been for fifteen years. Reopening the negotiation of NAFTA could be tantamount to ending NAFTA. This seems to be understood by the Obama administration; on April 20, 2009, U.S. trade representative Ron Kirk stated that the United States would not push to reopen NAFTA.

It is hard to predict NAFTA's future. There are differences in each country about what to do next. Focusing on Mexico and the United States (omitting Canada for the moment), the positions are to deepen the agreement (such as the customs union suggestion), look for additional mechanisms to promote North American integration (through infrastructure enhancement and a more regional approach to regulation), leaving things as they are (which is what is happening at the moment), or do away with the agreement altogether (something that the Mexican commentator Luis Rubio said would have dire consequences for Mexico).[35] Developments during the first hundred days of the Obama administration have complicated Mexico-U.S. trade relations. Mexico had obtained the right to retaliate against U.S. violation of the trucking provisions in NAFTA by a panel that ruled in Mexico's favor in 2001. The specific provision involved was the U.S. commitment to open access to Mexican trucks to bring cargo to destinations throughout the United States six years after NAFTA had come into effect—namely, on January 1, 2000.

The U.S. government, which was lobbied hard by the U.S. Teamsters Union, refused to put this agreement into effect, allegedly on grounds that Mexican trucks were unsafe and Mexican drivers would be inadequate because of their lack of mastery of English. The Mexican government chose not to retaliate despite the 2001 NAFTA panel ruling because of concern that tit-for-tat trade restrictions would damage Mexico's economic interests. President George W. Bush had supported a pilot program under which a limited number of Mexican trucks that had been precleared with respect to safety were given the right to bring cargo directly to destinations in the United States; these precleared trucks had the right not to have to unload the trailer carrying the cargo at the border for reloading onto a U.S. truck for transport the rest of the way.

This program was working well in the sense that the safety record of these trucks from Mexico was impeccable—indeed, better than the U.S. trucks carrying cargo from the border to the ultimate destination. However, the U.S. Congress voted to curtail funding for the pilot project, and Obama signed the legislation on March 11, 2009. Mexico retaliated by raising tariffs on many U.S. products coming into Mexico. That is the situation as this is written. Discussions are currently taking place within the U.S. administration, among the administration and the congress, and between the two governments on what happens next. The options are to live with the Mexican retaliation; perhaps to institute some counterretaliation by the United States, although it is not clear that grounds for this exist; restore the pilot program, even though this is just a modest substitute for the U.S. commitment in NAFTA; implement the NAFTA agreement as written on cross-border trucking; or negotiate something different from all these options. This trucking issue is discussed in greater detail in chapter 7 dealing with the border

Trade: From Closure to Opening

1949
- The U.S. Committee for Mexico of the National Foreign Trade Council urges Mexico to reconsider import control decrees and high import duties, among other things.

1954
- The Mexican peso is devalued from 8.65 to the U.S. dollar to 12.50 per dollar, a rate that remained stable for more than twenty years.

1956

- March 26–28: President Dwight Eisenhower of the United States, President Adolfo Ruiz Cortines of Mexico, and Prime Minister Louis St. Laurent of Canada meet in White Sulphur Springs, Montana, to discuss trade and other issues.

1960

- February 18: Mexico signs Montevideo Treaty, establishing the Latin American Free Trade Association (the Asociación Latino Americana de Libre Comercio, ALALC).

1964

- February 21–24: Presidents Lyndon Johnson of the United States and Adolfo López Mateos of Mexico meet in Palm Springs, California, to discuss mutual reduction of trade barriers.

1965

- May 20: The border industrialization program is announced. A key feature is the establishment of the maquiladora industry to provide employment for the expected return of Mexican farm workers following the termination of the bracero program by the United States in 1964.

1972

- October 23: President Luis Echeverría Alvarez of Mexico signs a decree requiring 60 percent Mexican ownership of auto parts manufacturers.
- November 4: Echeverría sends a bill to congress to limit the amount of foreign technology that Mexican companies can purchase, saying that it is important for "economic independence" for Mexico to develop its own technology.

1976

- August 31: The peso is devalued by 45 percent.

1977

- Mexico begins a program of reducing import quotas.

1980

- March: President José López Portillo, after a long negotiation with other contracting parties, announces that Mexico will not join the General Agreement on Tariffs and Trade (GATT).
- August 12: Mexico signs the new Treaty of Montevideo 1980, establishing the Latin American Integration Association (the Asociación Latino Americana de Integración, ALADI) and replacing the ALALC.

1981

- July: Import controls are gradually reimposed, reversing the 1977 reductions.

1982

- August: The debt crisis begins.

1983

- August 15: A decree is issued for the promotion and development of the maquiladora industry.

1986

- August: Mexico enters GATT and agrees as part of the process to eliminate the official price mechanism of customs valuation and to have a 50 percent import tariff ceiling.

1987

- November: A U.S.-Mexico framework agreement is reached, establishing a formal forum for discussion of trade and investment matters.
- November: Mexico eliminates the requirement for import licenses on many products.
- December: Mexico reduces the maximum tariff rate to 20 percent.

1988

- February 13: Presidents Ronald Reagan of the United States and Miguel de la Madrid of Mexico meet in Mazatlan to sign a new textile agreement under which the United States raises the Mexican quota by 6 percent. Agreements on telecommunications and civil aviation are also negotiated.
- July 1: Mexico switches merchandise classification from the customs cooperation nomenclature to the harmonized system of the World Customs Organization.

1989

- October 1–5: During a state visit to the United States, Presidents Carlos Salinas de Gortari and George H. W. Bush sign trade, steel, textile, investment, and environment agreements.

1990

- May 3: The decree promoting exports of high-exporting companies (the Empresas Altamente Exportadores, ALTEX) is published in the *Diario oficial de la federación*.
- May 3: Presidential decree establishes the program to allow imports for

producing goods to be exported (the Programa de Importación Temporal para Producir Articulas de Exportación, PITEX).

- June 12: Salinas and Bush meet to discuss a possible free trade agreement between the two countries.

1991
- June 12: NAFTA negotiations begin.

1992
- December 17: The presidents of Mexico and the United States and the prime minister of Canada sign the NAFTA agreement simultaneously but separately.

1993
- March 17: Negotiations begin on the parallel agreements to NAFTA on labor and the environment.
- December 20: The NAFTA agreement is published in the *Diario oficial.*

1994
- November 23: President-elect Ernesto Zedillo meets with President Bill Clinton in the White House to discuss trade and other issues.

1995
- May 11: Decrees are published in the *Diario oficial* amplifying ALTEX and PITEX.

1997
- June 25: Mexico imposes compensatory dumping tariffs on U.S. high fructose corn syrup imports, asserting that they were damaging Mexico's sugar producers. The antidumping duties were made definitive on January 23, 1998.

2000
- January 1: The agreement on trade-related intellectual property rights (TRIPS) negotiated in the Uruguay Round of GATT comes into full effect in Mexico.
- June 26: The Mexico–European Union free trade agreement is published in the *Diario oficial.*

2001
- April 22: A trilateral meeting between Presidents Vicente Fox and George W. Bush and Prime Minister Jean Chrétien takes place after the hemisphere summit meeting to discuss, among other subjects, approaches to strengthen NAFTA.

- May 3: Fox and Bush meet in Washington, D.C., to discuss trade and other issues.

2004

- March 5–6: Bush and Fox meet in Crawford, Texas, to discuss trade and other issues.
- November 21: Fox and Bush meet at the Asia Pacific Economic Cooperation (APEC) summit in Santiago, Chile, to discuss trade and other issues.

2005

- March 23: Leaders of Mexico, the United States, and Canada meet in Waco, Texas, and establish the Security and Prosperity Partnership (SPP) agreement as a vehicle to advance economic integration and other issues largely related to NAFTA.

2006

- The United States agrees, after sixteen years, to end the antidumping duties imposed on cement imports from Cementos Mexicanos (Cemex), bringing the import charge from twenty-six dollars to three dollars a ton. A key motivating factor for the United States was to reduce building costs on the Gulf Coast after Hurricane Katrina.
- March 30–31: The three North American leaders meet in Cancun and agree to form the North American Competitiveness Council.
- **2007**
- March 12–14: Bush and Calderón meet in Mérida, Yucatan, to discuss trade, among other issues.
- August 20–21: The three North American leaders meet in Ottawa to discuss trade and border issues.
- January 1: Final provisions of NAFTA conclude, ending tariffs on sensitive agricultural products, including corn and beans.
- April 21–22: Calderón and Bush and Prime Minister Stephen Harper meet in New Orleans for the fourth annual summit of the North American leaders, where they rejected critics' calls to renegotiate NAFTA.

2009

- March 11: President Barack Obama signs an Omnibus Appropriations Bill that, among other provisions, terminates funding for the pilot program allowing Mexican trucks to bring cargo to destinations throughout the United States.
- March 19: Mexico imposes import tariff increases ranging between 10

and 45 percent on eighty-nine products exported by the United States in
retaliation for the removal of funding in the spending bill Obama signed
for the pilot program for Mexican trucks.

- April 7: Approximately 140 businesses and organizations adversely
  affected by the Mexican trade retaliation ask Obama to adhere to U.S.
  NAFTA obligations.
- April 20: U.S. Trade Representative Ron Kirk states that Obama will
  not push to reopen NAFTA; rather, Obama will seek other options for
  strengthening the agreements on environmental and labor provisions.

Foreign Direct Investment and Finance
From Resistance to Welcome

Setting up a business is not as easy as we would like it to be.
— BRUNO FERRARI, 2008

Mexico's restrictions are clearly limiting FDI [foreign direct investment]. Easing them would be particularly beneficial since they are concentrated in infrastructure sectors that provide important inputs across the entire economy.
— OECD, 2007

exico's policy on seeking, or even tolerating, foreign direct investment (FDI) went hand-in-hand with the country's policy on trade. Taken together, they were the basis for the development-from-within philosophy practiced during the import-substitution years before 1982. It is possible to accept FDI for industrial development and then protect these foreign-owned activities from external competition. There was much of this in the automobile industry before NAFTA, for example, but allowing extensive foreign dominance in what can be called the commanding heights of Mexican manufacturing would have been inconsistent with the nationalism that accompanied import-substituting industrialization (ISI). Mexico, in the ISI years, wished either the state or its own nationals to dominate most phases of industrial development—from consumer goods, to intermediate products, and eventually to capital goods. As the timeline at the end of this chapter indicates, President Luis Echeverría Álvarez in 1972 even limited the amount of foreign technology that Mexican companies could buy in order to give an incentive to home-developed technology. Mexico's nationalism was defensive in nature. It fit the pattern of distancing the country from the United States in the same manner that trade policy did during the ISI years.

Manufactured-goods producers of all nationalities in Mexico were not encouraged to export during the ISI years and therefore had to rely heavily on the relatively small Mexican market for their sales. FDI, or equity investment, in petroleum and most natural gas operations was off limits to all private investors, foreign and domestic. FDI was also limited in extent of ownership in secondary petrochemicals, mining, and even the production of spare parts for vehicles. The purpose of the National Foreign Investment Commission (the Comisión Nacional de Inversiones Extranjeros, CNIE), established in 1973, was to screen foreign investment proposals under criteria designed to determine the permissible degree of foreign participation. Essentially the law was to *promote* Mexican investment and to *regulate* foreign investment. Regulation involved discussion between the prospective investor and officials of the CNIE, and this opened an obvious opportunity for corruption—and there was much of this.

The Years of Limiting Foreign Direct Investment

Foreigners were prohibited from owning banks in Mexico for about fifty years before NAFTA. The one exception was Citicorp, which had been allowed to do business in Mexico in 1929. The crisis of 1982 had a profound impact on Mexico's banking structure. On September 1 of that year, shortly before he was to leave office, President José López Portillo issued a decree bringing all banks except Citicorp and Banco Obrero (a union-owned bank) under the authority of the federal government. The affected banks were owned by Mexican nationals. The reason the president gave for his action was peculiar: "In the last two or three years . . . a group of Mexicans [. . .] supported and advised by the private banks, has stolen more money from our country than the empires that have exploited us since the beginning of our history. [. . .] They have robbed us [. . .] but they will not rob us again." López Portillo consulted with few people before he expropriated the banks, and there was no check on what he did. It was truly a dictatorial decision.[1]

In May 1989, President Carlos Salinas issued a decree, later approved by the legislature, to change the foreign investment law of 1973 to broadly allow FDI across sectors and to alter the procedures under which foreign investors could enter Mexico. In most sectors and for most projects foreign investors would no longer be required to negotiate with the CNIE, but approval would be automatic on registry if relevant criteria were met. If the relevant criteria were not met, approval would be automatic if not received within forty-five days of the application date. The opportunity for bribery in the negotiation for investment approval was therefore largely eliminated.

FDI was later opened further in the NAFTA negotiations, but Salinas's action in 1989 was a substantial opening to U.S. and other foreign investors. Thus two of the key cornerstones of Mexico's development policies that had prevailed for more than forty years after World War II—trade and investment policies—were swept away in a series of actions moving from development from within toward substantial economic interaction with the rest of the world. The changes deeply affected Mexico's relations with the United States, its most important trading partner and its largest source of FDI. The two key manifestations of defensive nationalism were disappearing. FDI into Mexico began to rise as the laws were modified in the 1980s to attract investment, rose even more as a consequence of the welcome provisions in NAFTA, and then rose even further in subsequent years as Mexico opened the banking system to foreign investment during the financial crisis at the end of 1994 (figure 3.1).

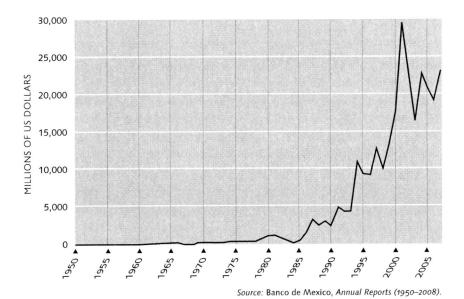

Source: Banco de Mexico, Annual Reports (1950–2008).

Figure 3.1. Foreign direct investment in Mexico, 1950–2007 (millions of US$)

Banking: From Domestic Privatization to Foreign Ownership

President Salinas, in May 1989, introduced legislation to privatize commercial banks. The actual negotiations began in June 1991, and the outcome did much to sully all of Mexico's privatization efforts. It was evident in Mexico when the 1991 privatization process started that the government's top priority was to maximize revenue.[2] Other privatizations at this time had a similar motive: to augment fiscal intake. More than half the revenue obtained from selling government-owned enterprises during the Salinas sexenio came from the sale of eighteen banks.[3] The Mexican government also signaled bidders for the banks—there were eighteen banks but four controlled seventy percent of bank assets—that they would not operate in a competitive environment and would not have to compete with foreign banks, which were not allowed to compete in the bank auctions.[4]

The government did not bring Mexico's accounting standards in line with generally accepted accounting standards. The banks were sold in six rounds of bidding between June 1991 and July 1992. All else being equal, the price paid for a bank rose in each bidding round. The average weighted bid-to-book ratio was 3.04, compared with a ratio of 1.89 in the United States in the 1980s and around 2.5 in Europe. Much of the money that the buyers put up to buy the banks was borrowed, some from the same banks they had just purchased.[5] Bank lending soared over the following three years, not matched by deposit increases. Much of the difference was obtained from loans, often in dollars from foreign banks, and many of the borrowers from the Mexican banks lacked enough income in dollars to service their loans. Nonperforming loans increased, many loans were restructured or renewed, and others were swapped for promissory notes from the deposit insurance system. If all these are taken into account, the nonperforming loan ratio in December 1996 would have been 52.6 percent.[6]

The entire process was sad: It started with a politically motivated government takeover of the banks in 1982. This was followed about a decade later by a reprivatization process designed to maximize fiscal revenue. To do this, the sources of funding for bank purchases were not scrutinized; the bid-to-asset ratio was maximized by promising the new bank owners that they would not face foreign competition. As a result, lending by the newly privatized banks became reckless leading to an astoundingly high ratio of nonperforming loans. All of this came to a head in 1994, when the Mexican financial structure found itself in serious straits from an overvalued exchange rate that led to the collapse of the peso at the end of 1994 and to the serious downturn of 6.9 percent in the Mexican economy in 1995, coupled with consumer price inflation that year of close to 40 percent (figure 3.2). Would the banks have failed even if the economy had not collapsed in 1994? Almost certainly, yes. This chapter explores the financial and exchange-rate policy of 1994 and then the bank rescue operation that took place essentially between 1995 and 1998.

The Interplay between Banking and Overall Financial Issues

NAFTA went into effect on January 1, 1994, and on the same day the Zapatista National Revolutionary Army (the Ejercito Zapatista de Liberación Nacional, EZLN) in the state of Chiapas declared war on the federal government. The year was replete with other dramatic events. On March 23 the PRI candidate to succeed Salinas, Luis Donaldo Colosio, was assassinated, and Ernesto Zedillo was chosen shortly thereafter by Salinas to replace Colosio as the candidate. Zedillo was considered a weak candidate, a person not clued in

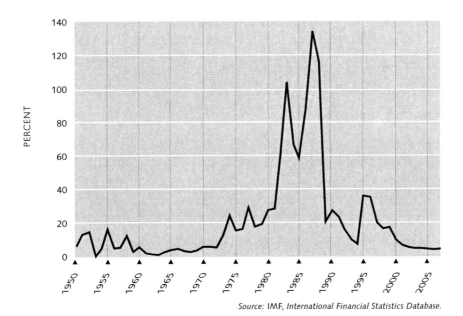

Source: IMF, International Financial Statistics Database.

Figure 3.2. Consumer price inflation in Mexico, 1950–2007

to the thinking of the PRI leaders. However, PRI control of the electoral structure was still overwhelming, and there was no question that Zedillo would be
elected president. The PRI's number-two official, José Francisco Ruiz Mas-
sieu, was assassinated on September 28.

Mexico was operating under what amounted to a fixed exchange rate in
1994, actually a band with a ceiling and a floor, and the policy was to keep rate
fluctuations within the band. The fixed exchange rate (or "fixed band") was
the anchor of the country's anti-inflation policy. Many Mexican economists
preferred that the exchange rate be allowed to float, but there were both political and practical reasons why Salinas and his minister of finance, Pedro Aspe,
opposed this. One key practical reason was concern that a devaluation of the
peso might weaken the already fragile commercial banks.[7] Salinas surely was
also aware that peso depreciation shortly after NAFTA went into effect would
give ammunition to anti-NAFTA groups who would assert that the purpose
of devaluation was to make Mexican goods and services more competitive
in the U.S. market. Finally, there was the political element that this would
weaken Salinas in the eyes of the public and damage the PRI coming into the
presidential elections of 1994.

The Mexican authorities sold dollars (that is, they bought pesos) in the
market to prevent a fall in the value of the peso. The dollars for this intervention came from selling *tesobonos*, dollar-indexed debt obligations of the government. By December 2004 the outstanding tesobonos exceeded Mexico's
level of foreign reserves; and with the evidently overvalued exchange rate, the
Mexican authorities found that the tesobonos could not be rolled over and
the demand for cashing them in for dollars exceeded the reserves Mexico had
to do this. The devaluation came on December 20, and the peso was allowed
to float on December 22. A new finance minister, Guillermo Ortiz Martínez,
was appointed on December 29. The Mexican authorities also announced
they would adopt measures to liberalize foreign participation in commercial
banks—a step that had been rejected in the privatization process of 1991–
1992 and was limited in the initial years of NAFTA. A year later the former
president Salinas issued a statement in which he said he had been made into
everybody's "favorite villain" (*villano favorito*). He referred to the devaluation
as the "error of December" (*el error de diciembre*). The first phrase was true,
but the second on the error of December was self-serving.[8]

The United States acted to provide a rescue loan to the Mexican government to the resolve the problem of funding the tesobono obligations and
provide security for foreign investors in Mexico. President Bill Clinton's jus-

tification for legislation that would provide a $40 billion loan guaranty to Mexico was phrased in terms of averting financial and economic danger in Mexico, but also to safeguard the economic future of the United States.[9] Republican leaders in the U.S. House and Senate supported the legislation, but it soon became clear that the Congress would not.[10] Consequently, the administration withdrew the legislation and opted instead to use funds from the Exchange Stabilization Fund (ESF), which was under the control of the U.S. Treasury, augmented by funds from the International Monetary Fund (IMF) and a number of central banks. The total guarantee amount was $48.8 billion, broken down as follows: $20 billion from the United States; $17.8 from the IMF; and the rest from various central banks on their own or working through the Bank for International Settlements. The use of the ESF for this purpose was legal, but extraordinary. The ESF had been established in 1934 to be used in arrangements with other central banks to stabilize the international exchange-rate system.

There were two main types of criticism of the loan guaranty: the first that it would not be repaid, and the second concerned moral hazard. The main safeguard against nonpayment risk was to set up an escrow account in the Federal Reserve Bank of New York, funded by foreign oil sales of Pemex, Mexico's national oil monopoly, to be used if Mexico failed to make interest or principal payments on time. There was never a need to draw on the escrow account. "Moral hazard" refers to third parties picking up the cost of failed investments. The argument in this case was that investors bought tesobonos to get higher returns than they could from other investments and that public funds, either from the United States or Mexico, should not be used to bail them out from the risks they took. This is a legitimate point; it is hard to justify allowing profits from risky investments to be private but then socialize the losses.[11]

President Zedillo put the Mexican economy under shock treatment in 1995, with full awareness that a large drop in GDP would ensue (figure 3.3). The hardships endured by the bulk of the Mexican population were severe. In 1996, however, Mexican GDP grew by about 5 percent. The sharp GDP decline in 1995 and the quick recovery in 1996 stand out. The Mexican authorities used $13.5 billion of the U.S. credit, but no more than $12.5 billion were outstanding at any one time. Total interest paid to the United States was $1.4 billion. Funds provided by the IMF were drawn down, but none of the credit lines provided by non-U.S. central banks was used.[12]

These financial and economic problems took place during NAFTA's first

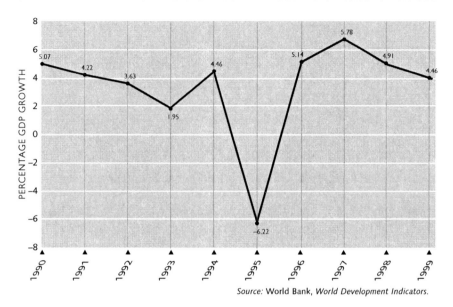

Source: World Bank, World Development Indicators.

Figure 3.3. Changes in Mexican GDP, 1990–1999 (annual percentage)

two years. It was not an auspicious start. Despite this, Mexico's increased access to the U.S. market under NAFTA contributed to the rapid recovery in just one year after the collapse in 1995. NAFTA had provisions both on facilitating FDI and on opening the Mexican banking system to U.S. banks. Focusing at this point on financial services, the following summarizes what Mexico granted in NAFTA. U.S. (and Canadian) commercial banks could increase their combined share from the 8 percent that existed in 1993 to 15 percent by the end of 1999. The share of individual foreign banks would be limited to 1.5 percent of the capitalization of the Mexican market, but all limitations would be eliminated by January 2000. If U.S. and Canadian banks obtained more than 25 percent of the market between 2000 and 2004, Mexico would be permitted to have a onetime moratorium for three years, thereby limiting further share increases until 2007. However, no single bank would be allowed to acquire more than a 4 percent share in the aggregate market; this provision was designed to protect the largest Mexican commercial banks from foreign takeovers. After ten years the only remaining restriction would be the implicit protection against foreign takeovers of large Mexican commercial banks. U.S. commercial banks were not allowed to establish branch banks in either

Mexico or Canada, but only subsidiaries, to conform to the restrictions that existed in the United States.[13]

Similar openings coupled with temporary restrictions were agreed to in NAFTA on foreign securities firms and insurance companies. The provisions in NAFTA were meticulously and arduously negotiated. The negotiators on both sides had their banking lobbies looking over their shoulders. Yes, open the system, but not too fast. Yes, protect the large Mexican commercial banks from foreign takeover. Still, the gains in NAFTA for foreign banks and other financial service companies were not negligible. The time limits on foreign ownership of commercial banks were eliminated when the authorities took account of the scope of Mexico's financial and economic crisis at the end of 1994. The best laid plans of defensive bankers then gave way because the Mexican economy faced dire realities. This is a point worth stressing because the same process of change during crisis took place in the trade and FDI fields after 1982 and in floating the peso in December 1994.

Dealing with the Banking Crisis

The Bank Fund for the Protection of Savings (the Fondo Bancario de Protección al Ahorro, FOBAPROA), a deposit insurance fund, came into being in 1995.[14] The fund was financed by contributions from the member banks. Its creation was prompted by concern about the growing level of nonperforming loans in what were still government-owned banks. Between late 1988 and late 1994 commercial bank lending to the private sector increased at an annual rate of 25 percent, mortgage loans by 47 percent a year, direct store credit for consumer durable goods at an annual rate of 67 percent, and credit card liabilities at a yearly rate of more than 30 percent. The fall in economic activity in 1995 worsened the situation of commercial banks as the value of shareholder deposits fell sharply in dollar terms; many borrowers lost their jobs and were unable to repay their loans. Others lost their homes as the cost of mortgages skyrocketed. At the end of 1994 the prime lending rate was almost 17 percent, rising to 58 percent in the middle of 1995, and did not fall below 20 percent until the second quarter of 1997. The Bank of Mexico, the central bank, had to make dollars available to commercial institutions so that they and their clients could pay foreign obligations. This was at a time when Mexico was so short of dollar reserves that the U.S. government felt obliged to step in with its rescue loan. The supervisory structure of the banks was weak and a new institution was created in May 1995, the Mexican National Banking and Securities Commission (the Comisión Nacional Bancaria y de Valores, CNBV), by fusing two existing agencies.[15]

A key aspect of the FOBAPROA program was to exchange delinquent loans held by banks for ten-year, zero-coupon government-issued bonds. The success of the program was mixed because even as bad loans were taken off the banks' balance sheets, past-due loans continued to increase. In January 1997 the CNBV required domestic banks to adopt a variant of the generally accepted accounting principles (GAAP) as one way to improve reporting of nonperforming loans. As the price of the rescue mounted, President Zedillo proposed in March 1998 that the costs of bank restructuring should be incorporated as government debt. This suggestion came after the 1997 congressional elections when the PRI, for the first time in modern Mexican history, lost its majority in the lower house of the congress and the opposition showed its power by refusing to grant the president authority to alter FOBAPROA's liabilities, some fifty-five billion dollars in private debt, and make them public debt of the federal government.

This was another example of moral hazard present in the large rescue loan in February 2005 that permitted the Mexican government to redeem its tesobono obligations. There were some horrible examples of Mexican bankers who had enriched themselves through self-lending, particularly at the end of 1994, when it was becoming evident that the peso would be devalued. The data also showed that Mexico's three largest banks—Banamex, Bancomer, and Serfin, which together controlled 53 percent of the assets of the banking system—held 48 percent of the government-issued FOBAPROA bonds. The price tag of the rescue was at least 15 percent of Mexican GDP, not as large as some other bank rescues in Latin America (in Argentina, Colombia, and Venezuela, for example) but substantial.[16]

The Mexican congress commissioned an independent audit of the bank rescue by Michael W. Mackey, a Canadian, before acting on Zedillo's proposal to nationalize the debt accumulated in the rescue operation. Mackey estimated in his report that the cost of the rescue was nearly sixty-four billion dollars. He also found that many of the loans transferred to FOBAPROA did not meet the criteria that had been established for this purpose. The final legislation was a compromise between Zedillo and the congress. It did not nationalize the cost of the banking rescue, but there was agreement to pay the annual costs in each year's budget.

The politically driven financial policy during 1994, the ensuing depression in 1995, the dismal performance of the privatized banks during this same period, and the bailout of many wealthy borrowers in the succeeding years combined to disillusion an already jaded middle class about Mexico's economic leadership. This distress contributed to the loss of the PRI majority in the Chamber of Deputies in 1997. The independence shown by the congress in the investigation of the bank rescue was a harbinger of the conflicted executive-legislative relations that have existed ever since. Mexico has three independent branches of government now that the legislature is not beholden to the executive. This separation of powers has not been conducive to making the structural reforms that can enable Mexico to achieve higher rates of economic growth, which implies that some change in executive-legislative interaction is inevitable. The financial problems contributed to the PRI's loss of the congress and subsequently of the presidency itself.[17]

Subsequent Investment and Banking Developments

The changes in Mexico's banking structure during the past twenty-five years have been extensive. There were twenty banks in Mexico after the bank seizures at the close of President López Portillo's six-year term—one foreign (Citibank), one domestic, and the remaining eighteen government-owned. In 1994, after the reprivatization, the numbers were thirty-one private domestic, two foreign, and zero government-owned. The figures at the end of 2005 were twelve private domestic, fifteen foreign-owned, and zero government-owned. Of the five largest commercial banks, only one is domestically owned (Banorte). The four largest foreign-owned banks in terms of share of assets are Citibank (whose main acquisition was Banamex), BBVA (the main acquisition was Bancomer), HSBC (the main acquisition was Bital), and Santander (the main acquisition was Serfin). The share of bank assets held by foreign banks was 83 percent in 2005.[18] A major conclusion of a number of studies on foreign bank ownership in developing countries is that they bring stability by lending more than domestic banks when confronted with financial crises. This has been the case in Mexico. One downside of foreign bank dominance in Mexico is that in-country geographic expansion is limited to wealthy urban areas without much spread to rural and poorer locations.[19]

In a 2007 IMF report, several points with respect to the country's banking situation stand out, especially after the turbulent situation of commercial banking in Mexico during the 1990s. The main conclusion is that "Mexico's banking system remains sound," which has contributed to the significant rebound in credit in the years before the U.S. credit crunch in 2009 when credit was curtailed globally. The report has a modest warning on the need to monitor the rapid growth in bank credit to households. It also notes that the mortgage market is flourishing, with little risk of problems similar to those that developed with subprime lending in the United States. The IMF pointed out two other issues regarding finance: (1) that the privately managed pension funds (Las Administradores de Fondos para el Retires, AFORES) have grown markedly and proved to be a stabilizing factor during financial market turbulence; and (2) that foreign reserves are about one and a half times total external debt on a residual maturity basis.[20]

Financial stability has been Mexico's outstanding economic strength thus far in the twenty-first century. Mexican government foreign and local currency debts were rated investment grade during this period by the three major credit-rating firms—Moody's, Standard & Poor, and Fitch. This means that U.S. pension funds can invest in Mexican government paper. FDI was attracted to Mexico because of this perception of financial stability. FDI has been consistently higher during recent years of financial stability than during the 1990s, when the financial situation was volatile. The annual average FDI inflow from 1994 through 2000 was about $11 billion, compared with an annual average inflow of about $22 billion from 2001 through 2007. The total stock of U.S. FDI in Mexico on a historical cost basis was $91.7 billion at the end of 2007.[21]

There was much internal criticism from informed economists that the Mexican treasury and central bank were overdoing their insistence on maintaining financial stability because this sacrificed economic growth. A few years later, however, despite its strong financial structure, Mexico was unable to escape unscathed from the U.S. financial and credit meltdown in the fall of 2008 and since. The repercussions of the U.S. credit crunch probably would have been worse if the banking system had not been strengthened earlier. In addition, Mexican financial stability during the early years of the twenty-first century—lack of fiscal deficits and conservative monetary policy—reduced the impact of the U.S. economic recession in 2008 on Mexico. FDI inflows were helped considerably by Mexican undertakings in NAFTA. Canada, Mexico, and the United States agreed in NAFTA to provide national treatment to investors in the other two countries—that is, treatment as favorable as each country grants its domestic investors. Each country also granted most-favored-nation (MFN) treatment to the other two—that is, treatment as favorable as any other foreign investor in the country. Mexico later concluded many other free trade agreements (FTAs) with comparable provisions.

The reason that Salinas turned to the United States when he proposed an FTA was his realization at the time that Western European countries were preoccupied with countries in Eastern Europe after the Berlin Wall had come down in 1989 and thus unlikely to provide much FDI to Mexico. Some twenty years later, however, Western Europe is providing substantial FDI to Mexico, thanks to the Mexico-European Union FTA that went into effect on July 1, 2000 (six and a half years after NAFTA went into effect) and coupled with Mexico's solid financial situation between 2000 and 2008, before Mexico's financial system was sideswiped by the U.S. credit crunch. The United States provided almost 50 percent of the $23 billion of FDI that Mexico received in 2007; the Netherlands provided about 15 percent (much of this probably originating in other countries); and Spain about 10 percent. As noted earlier, the Spanish banks Santander and BBVA have made large acquisitions in Mexico.

NAFTA investment provisions ban all new export-performance and domestic-content requirements. The agreement's trade-related investment measures (TRIMs) are more liberal than what was then under consideration in the Uruguay Round of the General Agreement on Tariffs and Trade (GATT). The dispute-settlement provisions effectively eliminated the Calvo Doctrine once largely ubiquitous in Latin America; the Calvo Doctrine had required that foreign investment disputes had to be resolved in the courts of the host country. NAFTA, by contrast, allows foreign investors to seek arbitral decisions in the World Bank's International Center for Investment Disputes (ICSID) or the UN Commission on International Trade Law (UNCITRAL). These arbitral awards can then be taken to the courts in any of the three countries. The economists Gary C. Hufbauer and Jeffrey J. Schott had high praise for NAFTA's investment provisions, with the notable exception of the primary energy sector as between Mexico and the United States.[22]

The pattern in Mexico's FDI and financial policies is similar to the policy that existed in trade policy—one of limitation or exclusion changing over the years because of changing circumstances. Until the 1980s FDI was tolerated, with considerable sector-by-sector limitations on the equity proportions that foreigners could hold. Each new foreign investment that was proposed had to be negotiated with a Mexican clearing institution, leaving considerable leeway for the mutual exchange of benefits between the investor and the screener. Much of this was eliminated in 1989. The 1982 debt crisis swept away many of the trade impediments of the ISI policy. The crisis also led to significant liberalization in the treatment of FDI. NAFTA's investment provisions then completed the job. The sequencing was one of drastic limits on FDI for many decades, then a change from grudging acceptance of FDI to seeking out prospective foreign investors, ending up with granting foreign investors the same treatment as that given to domestic investors. The entire transformation—from resistance, to partial acceptance, to assiduous seeking out of foreign investors—covered a period of more than half a century.

Mexico's policy toward commercial banking followed a similar pattern: rejection of foreign banks (with the exception of Citibank in 1929); not allowing foreign banks to bid in the auctions for privatizing commercial banks in 1991 and 1992; providing some concessions for foreign banks to operate in Mexico in the NAFTA negotiations, but deferring their ability for broad expansion in NAFTA's early years while simultaneously adding provisions to protect Mexico's most important banks from foreign acquisition; and then opening the banking system to foreign ownership at the height of Mexico's financial meltdown at the end of 1994. Mexican banking policy had the peculiar interlude of expropriation by President López Portillo in 1982, although the one foreign bank then in the country was spared this ordeal. The situation today is that foreign-owned banks control more than 80 percent of Mexico's banking assets.

The banking policy sequence is remarkably similar to that of opening Mexico to FDI generally—from the prohibition of foreign banking to the overwhelming dominance of foreign banks in twenty-five years, arbitrarily using the year of bank expropriation as the starting point. Economic-financial crises led to the changes in both cases. The United States was the main country that Mexican policymakers had in mind during the years of FDI restriction. The same was evidently true for the years of restrictive trade policy. Mexico kept its distance from the United States in both these areas only to witness increasing engagement between the two countries as the nature of the bilateral situation—and the global context—changed. From 2003 to 2007, Mexico's GDP grew by an average of more than 4 percent a year, a salutary departure from the lower growth of the previous two to three decades. The country's fiscal policy during these five years was conservative, inflation was largely under control, money-creation was modest, and the exchange-rate policy was largely one of clean floating that allowed the market to determine the peso-dollar relationship. FDI during these years flowed into the country in ample amounts. The banking system, as attested to by the IMF, was solid. There was much discussion among Mexico watchers in 2008 as to whether the country had "decoupled" its economy from that of the United States— whether Mexican economic growth would continue even as the U.S. economy declined.

Unfortunately, the U.S. financial meltdown during the latter half of 2008 and into 2009 has had a devastating impact on Mexico: there has been no decoupling. As this is written in the autumn of 2009, the consensus forecast is that Mexican GDP will decline by 7.5 percent in 2009. This is so despite the fact that Mexican banks did not engage much in subprime lending. However, exports to the United States have fallen sharply in 2009, the peso depreciated by about 40 percent with respect to the dollar, and there has been steady intervention by the Bank of Mexico to contain the slide. According to the Bank of Mexico, annual remittances from Mexican emigrants in 2008 fell for the first time since records have been kept; the decline was 3.6 percent to twenty-five billion dollars and is continuing to fall in 2009. Tourists are reluctant to travel to Mexico because of the level of drug violence. Concern about travel to Mexico is of course substantial in view of the H1N1 influenza virus; the extent to which this will depress the Mexican economy depends on the severity and recrudescence of the disease. The Mexican economy is going through an especially severe contraction and this time, unlike the slow economic growth during much of the past thirty-five years, the fault is not primarily Mexico's.

Foreign Direct Investment and Finance: From Resistance to Welcome

1897
- March 19: The first Ley de Instituciones de Credito is published, marking the beginning of private banks operating in Mexico.

1950s to 1970
- The Mexican policy of "stabilizing development" contributes to average GDP growth of 6 percent a year. Investment in this period is directed to high-priority operations.

1970
- Early in his term (December 1970–November 1976), President Luis

Echeverría Álvarez changes the policy to "shared development," designed to reduce inequality, accompanied by much inflationary spending, a fixed exchange rate during his term in office, and capital flight.

1972

- October 23: Echeverría signs a decree requiring 60 percent Mexican ownership of auto parts manufacturers and limiting the number of vehicle models that can be produced for each line.
- November 3: Echeverría sends a bill to congress to limit the amount of foreign technology that companies in Mexico can purchase.
- November 4: The Mexican government announces an end to foreign domination of the tobacco industry and establishes Tabamex, a company with 52 percent government ownership and the remaining 48 percent to be held equally by Mexican tobacco companies and farmers.

1973

- The Law to Promote Mexican Investment and Regulate Foreign Investment is passed and sets three classifications of foreign investment categories: (1) those reserved for the state, (2) those reserved for Mexican nationals, and (3) those in which minority foreign ownership is permitted. The law also establishes the National Foreign Investment Commission (the Comisión Nacional de Inversiones Extranjeros, CNIE) to evaluate foreign investment applications and sets up a foreign investment registry.

1975

- December 22: A mining law is passed (Regulatory Law of Article 27 of the Constitution) that restricts private and foreign access to the mining industry.

1982

- September 1: President López Portillo suspends convertibility of the Mexican peso and decrees the government ownership of private banks, sparing Citibank, the only foreign-owned bank at the time, and Banco Obrero, a union-owned bank.

1987

- November: A Mexico-U.S. framework agreement is reached for discussion of trade and investment matters of concern to both countries.
- December: The Pacto de Solidaridad Económica (PSE) is reached between government and private enterprises to curb wage and price inflation.

1989

- January: President Carlos Salinas de Gortari establishes the Pacto para la Estabilidad y Crecimiento Económico (PECE) as a continuation of the PSE, set up in 1987 by President Miguel de la Madrid.
- May 16: Salinas revises the 1973 foreign investment law and broadens the range of sectors open to foreign investment, allowing up to 100 percent foreign ownership in unrestricted sectors that account for two-thirds of Mexican GDP. The decree also makes investment automatic upon registry if it meets relevant criteria. If projects do not meet relevant criteria, review by the National Foreign Investment Commission must be made, and if not completed within forty-five days of the application date, the investment is approved.
- September 18: The privatization of Teléfonos de México (Telmex) is announced.

1990

- May: Salinas introduces legislation to privatize commercial banks. The Chamber of Deputies passes a bill that would allow up to 30 percent foreign ownership of eighteen commercial banks to be privatized.
- July: The Mexican government creates the Bank Fund for the Protection of Savings (the Fondo Bancario de Protección al Ahorro, FOBAPROA), a savings insurance mechanism, later involved in much investigation about the propriety of its actions. FOBAPROA implemented the banking bailout during the 1995 crisis.
- July 18: A law regarding credit institutions is passed, and Section IV, Article 122 of the law, makes FOBAPROA coverage universal for banks. Many banks used this legislation to take greater risks, which made the banking system more vulnerable to problems.

1991

- December: Approval of land tenure reforms change the legal status of the so-called *ejido* system, allowing private ownership of ejidos and giving them the right to enter into associations with private domestic and foreign firms.
- June: The Mexican government begins a series of six rounds of bidding that will last until July 1992 for the sale of the nationalized Mexican commercial banks.

1993

- November: The Mexican government announces a new foreign investment proposal replacing the 1973 code and uniting various regulatory changes imposed by decree by President Salinas.

- December 27: The new foreign investment law is published in the *Diario oficial*. While opening Mexico widely to foreign ownership and eliminating performance and minimum content requirements that previously existed, the state retains control of thirteen primary activities under the law, Mexican nationals retain sole ownership rights in various areas, and foreigners are limited to 49 percent ownership in others.

1994

- January 1: NAFTA goes into effect. On same day the Zapatista National Revolutionary Army declares war on the Mexican government in the state of Chiapas.
- December 20: Government foreign exchange reserves are largely depleted, and Mexico floats the peso, the value of which plummets. These actions lead to a sharp economic decline in Mexico in 1995.

1995

- February: The Mexican government removes restrictions on foreign bank ownership.
- February: A rescue package consisting of a line of credit of $48.8 billion is put together for Mexico after the country's 1994 financial crisis. The funds come from the Exchange Stabilization Fund of the U.S. Department of Treasury ($20 billion), the IMF ($17.8 billion), and the rest from other central banks, much of this made available through the Bank for International Settlements.
- May 12: An amendment to the 1993 foreign investment law is published in the *Diario oficial*.
- June 7: Another amendment to the 1993 foreign investment law is published in the *Diario oficial*.
- August: The government announces the debtor restructuring program (the Acuerdo de Apoyo Inmediato a Deudores de la Banca, ADE) under which bank loans are renegotiated at lower rates and subsidized by the government. Banks are instructed to suspend repossession and collection.

1996

- December 24: Another amendment to the 1993 foreign investment law is published in the *Diario oficial*.

1997

- January: Mexican banks are required to adopt generally accepted accounting practices (GAAP), which require that they disclose more financial information.

1998

- January 23: Another amendment to the 1993 foreign investment law is published in the *Diario oficial*.
- Mexico negotiates Reciprocal Investment Promotion and Protection Agreements with Austria, the Belgium-Luxemburg Economic Union, France, Germany, and the Netherlands.
- March: President Ernesto Zedillo proposes to the Mexican congress that the cost of bank rescues, about $55 billion, be incorporated into the national debt.

    The Mexican Chamber of Deputies hires independent auditor Michael Mackey to report on all transactions conducted by FOBAPROA. The report turns out to be controversial in that it points to apparent corruption and mismanagement by government agencies.
- December: Congress agrees on formal measures to reform the banking system, accepting and reworking many of Zedillo's suggestions. The congress agrees that the annual cost of the banking sector rescue would be paid for by the government out of each year's budget. A letter of intent from the Mexican government to the IMF outlines the reforms and restructuring efforts.

1999

- January 19: Another amendment to the 1993 foreign investment law is published in the *Diario oficial*.

2000

- March 28: Moody's upgrades Mexican bonds to investment grade. Other rating agencies, Standard & Poor's and Fitch, follow suit in subsequent years.

2001

- June 4: The Law of Investment Companies is published in the *Diario oficial*, designed to give small and medium-sized industries better access to financial credit and to provide better access to securities markets.

2007

- December: In the report "Mexico 2007 Article IV Consultation," the IMF states that Mexico's financial system continues to strengthen and the banking system remains sound.

Narcotics
Effect of Profits from U.S. Consumption

It is our [developing country's] men and women who die first in combating drug trafficking; it is our communities that are the first to suffer from violence; our institutions that are first to be undermined by corruption.
—PRESIDENT ERNESTO ZEDILLO, 1998

Skeptics and advocates of drug legalization have long argued that our fight against drugs is hopeless, but the results tell us yet again that our Nation's fight against drugs is anything but. In fact, we are winning.
—U.S. NATIONAL DRUG CONTROL STRATEGY, 2008

U.S. efforts to curtail drug use have both internal and external venues—a "war on drugs" at home and pressure on foreign countries to curtail their production of field crops (such as coca, opium poppies, and marijuana) and laboratory preparations (such as methamphetamine) and to employ their military and police to interdict narcotics before they enter the United States. The costs, both monetary and personal, are enormous in both countries. These policies have been in effect for decades, and questions have been raised about their effectiveness for all this time. Reports issued by the U.S. and Mexican governments describe many temporary successes—drug seizures, arrests of kingpins, and hectares of crops destroyed—but the more prevalent assessment is that the U.S. anti-narcotics program has been a long-term failure.[1]

Jeffrey Davidow, a former U.S. ambassador to Mexico, has written that the United States for many years centered its entire relationship with Mexico on the issue of narcotics.[2] The foreign policy scholar María Celia Toro has made the point that as the 1980s unfolded, drug trafficking became the most important source of Mexico-U.S. conflict.[3] If one merely skims through the timeline at the end of this chapter, the number of times that the U.S. government acted unilaterally to push Mexico into greater action to deter narcotics coming from or through its territory into the United States jumps out. These actions included the two Operation Intercepts, the process under which the U.S. president had to certify that Mexico was cooperating fully with the United States to combat narcotics traffic in order not to lose U.S assistance in other areas, and Operation Casablanca.[4] The United States pushed its drug addiction problem on Mexico in much the same manner that Mexico pushed its human emigration problem on the United States. In each case the country faced a domestic problem it was unable to correct—lack of adequate job-creation in Mexico and excessive drug consumption in the United States—and argued that the bilateral resolution it sought benefited both countries.

Domestic Aspects of U.S. Antidrug Policy

Detailing all of the agencies and elements of U.S policy used over the years to combat drug consumption is the subject of another book. For the purposes here, U.S. policy is based on imprisonment of drug offenders—leaders of major drug-trafficking organizations, neighborhood vendors and buyers, and perennial and casual drug users—to an extent unmatched anywhere else in the world. At any single point in time there are roughly half a million drug violators behind bars, about a quarter of the total U.S. prison and jail population. Consider this: the United States has 5 percent of the world's population, but 25 percent of the world's prisoners.[5] The U.S. imprisonment rate for drug offenders was 149 per 100,000 of the population in 1995, compared with, say, France, where the rate is 95 per 100,000 of the population for *all* prisoners. Another important consideration: nonwhites make up almost 75 percent of U.S. drug offenders in prison.[6]

Mexican commentators have sometimes complained that much is being asked of Mexico in its antidrug operations because the United States is not doing enough to curtail its own drug consumption. The extent of imprisonment for U.S. drug offenses makes it evident that this charge is false. The United States, however, may be doing the wrong things to curtail drug consumption. The analysis in a 2006 article in the *Journal of Political Economy* comes to precisely this conclusion.[7] Three key points are made: (1) imprisonment and other punishments lead to higher prices, but if demand for the product is inelastic, this leads to an increase in spending on illegal goods like drugs; (2)

the social costs exceed the social gains by making consumption illegal for an inelastic product like drugs; and (3) excise taxes can be a much more effective way to reduce consumption whatever the elasticity of demand, but these taxes are hard to apply on an illegal product. The noted development economist Deepak Lal wrote in a letter to the *Financial Times* that the United States should deal with drug addicts "by treating them as patients not criminals."[8]

Direct U.S. federal drug control spending has been about $26 billion a year.[9] President George W. Bush's request for fiscal year 2009 was $14.1 billion; broken down by functions, the amounts were $3.8 billion for interdiction, $3.7 billion for domestic law enforcement, $3.4 billion for treatment with research, $1.6 billion for international, and $1.5 billion for prevention with research. Actual monetary expenditures are much higher after taking into account the cost of imprisonment of five hundred thousand drug offenders at any given time. The major drugs for which federal arrests are made are cocaine in its various forms, marijuana, heroin, and methamphetamine. Twenty percent of those arrested are juveniles and the number of youth arrests rose more than 80 percent between 1991 and 1997.[10] There are no reliable data on the effect on the lives of arrested juveniles, or others, or on the consequences for their families. The U.S. strategy of mass arrests for drug offenses imposes a high and essentially incalculable cost on U.S. society, and yet it goes on and on. The narcotics scholars Jonathan Caulkins and Peter Reuter have suggested that imprisonment for drug offenses should be cut in half; they admit there is nothing behind the precise size of the cut other than that they want it to be dramatic.[11]

The widespread belief that U.S. antidrug policy has not been successful has led naturally to suggestions for policy modification. The most dramatic proposals are to legalize drug use, similar to what was done when alcohol prohibition was abolished in December 1933. This would eliminate most of the imprisonment and probably reduce the violence that accompanies the sale of prohibited products. The illegal drugs attract prices well above what market supply and demand would dictate precisely because they are prohibited. Many prominent Americans have supported this position, including Milton Friedman, George Shultz, and William Buckley. One notch down is support for the legalization of less dangerous drugs, primarily marijuana. There is no agreement as to whether marijuana is a so-called gateway drug whose use is a stepping-stone to harder drugs (this is the official position of the U.S. government), or whether the use of marijuana peaks when a drug user is in his or her twenties and then drops off in subsequent years. Many countries have criminal penalties for the use of the most lethal drugs, but not for marijuana. Swiss voters in November 2008, for example, approved a proposal to make permanent a program that supplies heroin to addicts unable to rid themselves of the habit.[12]

The main argument against legalization of drug use is that this would lead to greater addiction. Joseph Califano, a former secretary of Health, Education, and Welfare, is ardently opposed to legalization because he believes this would condemn drug addicts, particularly young African-Americans and Latinos, to a lifetime of drug use. It is not clear if this means that they would suffer even more than they do today from high imprisonment rates. His pithy argument is that "drugs are not dangerous because they are illegal; they are illegal because they are dangerous."[13] The evidence is ambiguous that drug legalization would lead to greater addiction. Alcohol consumption rose after prohibition was ended, but the evidence is that the increase in consumption started while prohibition was still in effect.[14] If the drug-trafficking organizations were removed from the scene because drugs were legally available, one would expect consumption to rise from the lower price. Although demand for these products is price inelastic, it is not completely so. In any event, if the government distributed drug products through its own stores, as alcohol is still marketed in many states, or sanctioned distribution by private companies, the price could be raised through excise taxes—a policy that economists Gary Becker, Kevin Murphy, and Michael Grossman have argued is superior to the coercion policy that now exists.[15] The money saved from abandoning the current policy of arrest and imprisonment could be used for more education about the harmful effects of drug use and much more drug treatment could be provided than now takes place. These measures would also have some effect in lowering consumption, as it does for tobacco.

Drug legalization proposals, partial or complete, can be left here. The argument is often heard in the United States that legalization is a better option than criminalization and imprisonment, but the public is not prepared to accept this. The evidence from a poll by Zogby International in September 2008 supports this contention.[16] This is the same argument that is used in Mexico for not allowing joint ventures between Pemex, Mexico's national oil company, and private investors—that this might facilitate more efficient exploration for and production of oil, but the public would not accept it. These are sacred cows—decriminalization of drug use in the United States and permitting private equity investment in oil in Mexico—that cannot be dispassionately discussed in the respective countries.

Domestic Aspects of Mexican Antidrug Policy

Drug trafficking was not an important issue for Mexico before the 1970s.[17] This does not mean that the subject was neglected. Mexico supported the Hague International Opium Convention in 1912, and during the following years commercialization of the main narcotics produced in Mexico was formally prohibited—opium in 1920 and poppy in 1926. Mexico did not produce cocaine, and marijuana output was mostly sent north of the border.[18] Consumption of these drugs in Mexico was not high. Mexico, consequently, had little incentive to cooperate with the United States in drug interdiction or crop destruction. The dominant view in Mexico was that the drug-trafficking problem arose from the inability of the United States to control its domestic demand for heroin, cocaine, and marijuana; the dominant U.S. view was that the Mexican government failed to make effective efforts to control the supply of drugs.[19]

Operation Intercept, launched by the United States in September 1969, by dramatically intensifying vehicle inspection at the border with Mexico, was designed to pressure Mexico to raise the priority of its antidrug efforts. The operation also served to strengthen the Nixon administration's domestic political profile on antidrug measures.[20] The Mexican government reacted indignantly to Operation Intercept because of its adverse effects on tourism and exports. But it also responded as the U.S. authorities wished by entering into an agreement with the United States called Operation Cooperation. Nevertheless, the Mexican government's deeper sentiment remained what it had been before—that the U.S. pressure on Mexico was designed to deal with what was primarily a domestic U.S. problem. This view changed over time as drug consumption in Mexico grew. Mexican president Carlos Salinas explained Mexico's policy of cooperation with the United States to combat drug use and trafficking in an address to a joint session of the U.S. Congress on October 4, 1989: "Mexico views the fight to end drug trafficking as a matter of national security, a concern for the health of Mexican youth, and an act of solidarity with the community of nations."

Celia Toro, who has done much research on Mexican drug policy, has written that Mexican drug policy was largely determined by U.S. policy. She goes on to argue that the policy pushed on Mexico has simply not worked.[21] The core antidrug effort in Mexico in the 1970s was Operación Cóndor, in which Mexico increased funding and doubled the size of its police force for the operation. The centerpiece of the program was aerial spraying with the herbicide paraquat to destroy the narcotic crops in the field. The herbicide and the aircraft for this operation were provided by the United States. According to Jorge Chabat, a Mexican scholar on narcotics issues, the operation succeeded in reducing the production of poppy and marijuana plants.[22] Chabat also noted that the military, which had contributed modestly in previous Mexican antinarcotic campaigns, collaborated in the so-called permanent Operation Condor campaign. The objective of the earlier U.S. pressure imposed by Operation Intercept in 1969 was to get Mexico to use aerial spraying to destroy drug crops—and this is precisely what was done in Operation Condor. The operation came to an end in the mid-1980s largely because of the ecological damage from the spraying.

Mexico's antidrug policy has three major shortcomings. The first is that consumption of hard drugs has increased over the years. In a lengthy story in the *Washington Post* on March 16, 2008, Manuel Roig-Franzia discussed the transformation of Rosarito Beach, a town about twenty minutes travel time south of Tijuana that drew many tourists and surfers and then became a key transshipment point for sending drugs to the United States. According to the article, the drug dealers controlled the town and it was impossible for youths to avoid drug dealers whose children went to school with them. In the same article Roig-Franzia, citing Victor Clark, a Tijuana human rights and drug expert, wrote that drug addiction in Tijuana had doubled from one hundred thousand in 2004 to two hundred thousand in 2007. The Mexican authorities could no longer argue that their young people were different from those in the United States in that they had not caught the affliction of drug addiction.[23]

The second problem has been the widespread corruption of Mexico's many police forces. The money offered by Mexico's large drug-marketing operators was much too tempting for generally low-paid police officials to resist. It was commonplace for them to be offered double what the various governments, federal, state, and local, paid them—and the alternative to joining with the drug dealers was often death. It was not just low-level police who succumbed to bribes. As detailed in the timeline at the end of the chapter, General Jesús Gutierrez Rebello was arrested and later convicted in the late 1990s for protecting a leading drug dealer. President Felipe Calderón purged 284 police commanders from all thirty-one states and the federal district and instituted drug polygraph and other tests for their replacements.[24] This apparently was not enough, however. In May 2007 a Federal Support Military Corps was established in Mexico's defense ministry, and twenty-five thousand to thirty thousand military personnel were assigned to assist the civilian police in combating drug crimes. Although this was not the first time that military personnel were deployed in the antidrug campaign, the numbers were impressive. The newspaper *El universal* found in a survey that 91 percent of those polled favored military involvement.[25] Military personnel are not immune to bribes—witness the case of General Gutierrez Rebello—but they have a better record for professionalism than the police.

The third problem with Mexico's antidrug policy is the violence associated with drug dealing. The number of people killed by drug violence in 2006 and 2007 is reported to be forty-eight hundred. The killings during 2008 exceeded fifty-three hundred. They stem from drug cartel competition to control various parts of the U.S. market, but many innocent individuals are caught up in the process. So too are police and military personnel. For example, within eight hours of his acceptance to be chief of police in Nuevo Laredo on June 8, 2005, the new chief was murdered.[26] On March 3, 2008, soldiers and police battled drug-traffickers in a five-hour shootout in Tijuana during which one policeman and one suspected gang member were killed. The next day the bodies of five youths who were handcuffed and sprayed by bullets were found in Tijuana.[27]

Journalists are fearful about publishing stories about drug-related killings because it can cost them their lives. In the past fourteen years thirteen journalists were slain in direct relation to their reporting on drug killings, and another fourteen were murdered under unclear circumstances.[28] As a consequence, journalists practice much self-censorship, or if their publishers are courageous enough to print stories on drug-related crimes, the articles are left unsigned.[29]

The Mexican drug cartels gathered strength after the mid-1980s, when drug traffickers shifted away from their previous route to the United States through the Caribbean to Florida because U.S interdiction efforts made this approach precarious. The traffickers most commonly then used the direct route from Colombia (for cocaine), through Central America and Mexico into the United States. There are a number of Mexican cartels: the Gulf Cartel that historically operated in the northeastern state of Tamaulipas; the Sinaloa

Cartel, which operates in many Mexican states at or near the U.S. border; and the Juárez Cartel, sometimes referred to as the Arellano Felix Organization, which apparently has declined in importance compared to the Gulf and Sinaloa cartels. Other drug marketers include the Beltran Leyva Organization, which split off a few years ago from the Sinaloa Cartel. The relative power-er of these marketers shifts over time. The cartels have their own enforcers known as *sicarios*. The Gulf Cartel had its own disciplined enforcers known as Zetas, and the Sinaloa Cartel has its enforcers known as Negros. The Zetas in particular have become a threat to national security, and their operations extend beyond the area of the Gulf Cartel.[30]

It is not exaggeration to say that a war is going on between the Mexican government and the drug cartels and their enforcers. Pitched battles between the military and police on the part of the government and the cartels and their enforcers are reported regularly in the press. Mexico is also plagued by kidnappings for ransom, and even killings after ransom is paid. The combination of kidnappings and drug violence are the most serious problem facing the Calderón government.[31] Chabat believes that if the Mexican state is unable to provide security, other national tasks cannot be performed.[32] Other experts argue that if this violence cannot be brought under control, Mexico will not be able to function as a democratic state.[33]

The U.S.-Mexico Antidrug Relationship

Once Mexico became the dominant route for the movement of narcotics to the United States, two other developments were probably inevitable: (1) Mexicans would become more addicted to drug use, especially in the transshipment areas because so many drugs would be available; and (2) Mexican cartels would become the dominant national cartels controlling the shipments to the United States. It is unclear what actions, if any, the Mexican government took to explicitly prevent these developments. Mexico must deal with its own addiction problem but will not be able on its own to eliminate the horrible consequences of the vast sums of money available to its drug lords from narcotic sales in the United States. The amount of money the drug cartels earn from narcotics sales in the United States cannot be precisely determined. In a report to the U.S. Congress, Colleen Cook of the Congressional Research Service has said that estimates range from $13.6 billion to $48.4 billion a year. John Walters, the director of the U.S. Office of National Drug Control and

Policy, gave the figure of $14 billion a year taken in by the Mexican drug king-pins for the sale of methamphetamine, heroin, cocaine, and marijuana in the United States. He stated that marijuana is the "bread-and-butter" drug whose sales account for more than 60 percent of the total.[34] The drug policy expert Mark Kleiman gave a figure of $50 billion a year as the take of drug-dealing industries from all locations, not just Mexico.[35]

Even if the figure is at the low end—say, fifteen billion dollars a year—what can the Mexican authorities do to counteract the bribery and the violence made possible by this large sum? Mexico spends more than five billion dollars a year in its antidrug efforts, but the total figure is hard to calculate because different outlays are in many places in the budget, under various headings. Perhaps the wages of the police and military dedicated to the antidrug pro-gram could be increased to make them less vulnerable to bribery, but this would set off pressure for public employee wage increases generally and trig-ger higher inflation. Mexico is a developing country and trying, on its own, to outbid the drug cartels is not a feasible solution. Probably the best the Mexi-cans can hope for is that if their government wages total war against the drug traffickers, the route for drug sales into the United States would move to an-other location—as happened earlier with the Caribbean route into Florida.[36]

The enforcers for the drug cartels are well supplied with such weapons as powerful AR-15s, AK-47s, Colt .38 supers, and others, most of which come from the United States.[37] In many head-to-head battles the drug cartel enforc-ers are better armed than the Mexican police. The military are generally well armed, and this is one reason so many soldiers are being used today in the antidrug campaign. Mexican authorities have complained to the U.S. govern-ment about the flow of arms from the United States into Mexico, thus far with little effect. The United States has never ratified the Inter-American Conven-tion Against the Illicit Manufacturing of and Trafficking in Firearms, Am-munition, Explosives, and Other Related Materials (known as CIFTA) that entered into force in 1998 and has been ratified by nearly all members of the Organization of American States. The agreement was signed by the United States in 1997 and has languished in the Senate ever since.[38] President Barack Obama stated on April 19, 2009, that he will seek ratification of CIFTA. The Senate has not acted as of this writing in September 2009.

The history of Mexican-U.S interaction in combating drug trafficking has exhibited a repetitive pattern: the United States pushes Mexico to take action to destroy and interdict crops, and Mexico reacts, partially at times and more fully on other occasions. Since the mid- to late 1980s, the constants have been large sales of narcotics coming from Mexico into the United States and a significant flow of money accruing to the Mexican drug dealers. The amounts moving in each direction—narcotics to users in the United States and money to drug dealers in Mexico—vary by circumstances in any year, but the movements have been substantial during this period. There are periodic incidents that heat up the relationship. One of the most significant was the murder of DEA special agent Enrique Camarena in 1985, which led to the second U.S. Operation Intercept designed to punish Mexico. It also led, about five years later, to the U.S.-arranged kidnapping of Humberto Álvarez Machâin, who was believed to be involved in the torture of Agent Camarena. The Camarena murder was a major event, and U.S. exasperation was profound and long-lasting.

The year after the murder the U.S. Congress instituted the policy of requiring the president to certify that Mexico and other countries were cooperating fully with the United States in combating narcotraffic. If not, the penalty would be to cease giving aid to the country, directly or indirectly (such as voting against loans from international financial institutions). Mexico and Latin America generally resented this policy because of the sense that the United States created the problem, but the blame was being placed elsewhere. There has been some drama over the years as the U.S. president's certification decision had to be made, but Mexico has never been decertified.

Cooperation often lapsed and later resumed between the two countries. In his address to a joint session of the Mexican congress in 1989, President Salinas promised all-out cooperation with the United States in the fight against drug trafficking; he held back on one point, however, saying that the fight in our country is exclusively ours and therefore "there will be no joint military operations on our soil." Then, during the administration of President Zedillo, the evidence that General Gutierrez Rebello was cooperating with a particular drug cartel became public and the U.S. reaction was again one of exasperation. The U.S. lack of trust about sharing sensitive information with Mexican antidrug and anti–money laundering institutions was again evident in the late 1990s.

When President Vicente Fox addressed a joint session of the U.S. Congress in September 2001, he asked that legislation be passed to suspend drug certification requirements, stating that "trust requires that one partner not be judged unilaterally by the other." There was considerable cooperation on antidrug activities between the two countries during the six years of the Fox administration. However, as a report in late 1994 from the Congressional Research Service to the U.S. Congress put it: "Despite impressive eradication efforts, the estimated production in Mexico of opium poppy gum and marijuana increased significantly in the last year for which reporting is complete."[39]

While U.S. exasperation with the defects it saw in Mexico's antidrug operations was repeatedly manifested, the reverse occurred in 2007 and 2008. In an interview with the *Washington Post* published on March 23, 2007, the Mexican ambassador Arturo Sarukhan said that the United States has contributed "zilch" to Mexico's efforts to combat the problem both countries have in dealing with criminal narcotics gangs.[40] This was clearly part of a concerted effort by the Mexican government. When Presidents Calderón and Bush met in Mérida, in the Mexican state of Yucatan, in the same month, Calderón took what the *Economist* called an "unusual step for a Mexican president" in asking Bush to provide help with fighting the drug cartels.[41] Bush said that he would ask Congress to approve $500 million for the first year of the Mérida Initiative as the first part of the multiyear assistance program of $4.1 billion. There was some debate in the Senate about the amount of the first year's appropriation, but in the end it came to $400 million for Mexico and $65 million for Central American countries. The assistance will provide training and equipment.

However, Senate consideration of the legislation exhibited the fragility of the bilateral antidrug effort. In its initial proposal the Senate Judiciary Committee, at the urging of such nongovernmental organizations as Amnesty International and Human Rights Watch, imposed conditions to monitor possible human rights violations of Mexico's security forces in their antidrug efforts. The response to this from the Mexican side was that it would not accept the assistance if it was tied to oversight of the Mexican military by U.S. civilian monitors. One Mexican argument was that the United States asks for too much in its provision of $400 million, less than 10 percent of Mexico's own expenditures in what is supposed to be a cooperative effort. The problem was essentially finessed in the final legislation, but the Mexican press later reported that an auditing position was created in the U.S. embassy in Mexico City precisely to monitor the costs and efficiency of the aid under the Mérida Initiative. According to one report, $340 million of the $400 million would be made available after the U.S. Department of State presented a plan for their expenditure, and the remaining $60 million would depend on a report dealing with the protection of human rights in the antidrug operation.[42] It all smacks of President Ronald Reagan's comment about working with the Soviet Union: "trust, but verify."

The Sequencing of Antidrug Cooperation

The U.S. government, early in the process of seeking Mexican action to fight drug addiction in the United States, chose to impose pressure to accomplish this. Operation Intercept in 1969 was a bludgeon—it was a message to Mexico to either destroy its narcotic crops or have its border with the United States closed. There were numerous messages of this type over the ensuing years—cooperate or else, the "or else" being further closure of the border, unilaterally searching out money laundering in Mexico, kidnapping a Mexican citizen for trial in the United States, and asking the U.S. president to certify that Mexico was cooperating in the antidrug effort. The word "exasperation" is frequently used to describe U.S. reaction to increasing flows of drugs from and through Mexico and Mexican police corruption in dealing with this problem. U.S. police undoubtedly were less corrupt than the many Mexican police forces, but the United States had little success in interdicting drug shipments into its territory. The ability to close down the Caribbean route for drug shipments did not reduce U.S. narcotic imports, but rather resulted in a route change through Central America and Mexico. The United States often gave the impression that it was annoyed with Mexico for being located where it was.

However, antidrug cooperation between Mexico and the United States did prosper at various times. The high point was Operation Condor under which Mexico significantly increased its police and military forces in drug interdiction efforts and agreed to herbicide spraying of illegal drug crops for many years until the concern over environmental damage from the spraying program became too great. The Mexican Supreme Court ruled that Mexicans could be extradited to the United States for drug crimes, and many extraditions followed. To deal with police corruption in the fight against drug cartels, President Calderón reformed the police structure. When the results of this action were modest, he substantially increased the military's role in the effort. The Mexican embassy in Washington, D.C., issues regular press releases on drug seizures, for example, of cocaine in the state of Colima and marijuana throughout the country, extraditions of drug criminals to the United States (eighty as of November 2007), allocation of additional funds for addiction treatment, apprehensions of members of Los Zetas and seizures of millions of dollars from them, and intelligence-sharing with the United States.[43]

There has been considerable criticism in Mexico of the Mexican government for being too docile in dealing with U.S. demands in the antidrug programs. One argument was that U.S. policy forced Mexico into overcriminalizing the drug market.[44] The Mexican congress in 2006 enacted legislation to drop criminal charges for possession of small amounts of drugs; the motive was to concentrate antidrug efforts on big-time smugglers and dealers. President Fox vetoed the legislation under pressure from Washington and mayors of U.S. border cities.[45] Mexico increased its antidrug cooperation with the United States not merely in response to U.S. demands, although this coercion played a large role in determining Mexican policy, but also because its own drug addiction problem was increasing. Mexico showed considerable backbone in 2007, however, when Calderón told Bush in Mérida that cooperation from the United States was lacking. After the Mérida Initiative legislation was approved by the U.S. Congress, Jeffrey Davidow commented: "It's a different ballgame now. It is a question of Mexico asserting itself as a partner and not as a supplicant."[46]

Mexican presidents have justified their antinarcotics cooperation with the United States as a matter of defending national security. Yet until Calderón assumed office at the end of 2006, there had been little direct confrontation with the drug cartels and their militias. This confrontation is now taking place, and the violent consequences have probably made Mexico's antinarcotics program its most important current national security issue. The United States also looks on its antinarcotics efforts as a national security issue, as the very name of the program—the "war on drugs"—demonstrates. However, the U.S. government did little to support Mexico in its antinarcotics efforts until Calderón shamed Bush into doing this when the two met in Mérida. The United States has been more focused on limiting clandestine entry from Mexico, such as by construction of a fence along the border, than on helping Mexico deal with its security problem.

It is hard to forecast how smooth Mexico-U.S. antidrug cooperation will be in the future because there is no indication that U.S. drug consumption will diminish over time or that Mexico will cease being the main point for drugs entering the United States. The problems between the two countries will persist as long as drug marketers in Mexico can generate the large income that they receive for supplying an illegal product in great demand in the United States.

Narcotics: Effect of Profits from U.S. Consumption

1948
- The *gran campaña* against drug use in Mexico is officially launched.

1961
- Both Mexico and the United States sign the Single Convention on Narcotic Drugs. Mexico signs under pressure from the United States.
- Mexico acquires five hundred thousand dollars' worth of aircraft, helicopters, jeeps, weapons, and other equipment needed by drug enforcement agencies in 1961 and 1962.

1969
- September: The United States launches Operation Intercept, deploying more than two thousand customs and border patrol agents along the Mexican border to intensify vehicle inspection. The underlying purpose of the operation was to raise the priority of antidrug efforts in Mexico. The Mexican government protested, noting the immense traffic jams and adverse impact on its tourist income and exports from the operation.
- October 11: After the diplomatic fiasco of Operation Intercept, it is replaced by Operation Cooperation between the two countries.

1970–1975
- After Turkey implements a crackdown on heroin production under pressure from the United States, Mexico becomes a large player, providing about 70 to 80 percent of heroin intake in the United States by 1975.

1974
- January–February: Mexico cooperates with the newly established U.S. Drug Enforcement Administration (DEA) in several operations to combat heroin traffic.

1975
- November: After a secret meeting between Mexican and U.S. officials, Mexico launches Operation Condor. The size of the federal police force is doubled, and military personnel are added in the country's antidrug campaign. The centerpiece of the operation is an aggressive aerial-spraying campaign with the highly toxic herbicide paraquat, using

mostly U.S.-provided aircraft, to destroy growing fields. The program terminated in the mid-1980s, partly on ecological grounds and partly because of diminishing effectiveness, but largely because of corruption in the Mexican agency that was in charge of the spraying efforts.

1984

- The Report of the Select Committee on Narcotics Abuse and Control submitted to the Ninety-eighth U.S. Congress found that Mexico was the only country fulfilling its "obligation" to eradicate cultivation of illicit narcotic crops in its territory, and that this was of enormous benefit to the people of the United States.

Mid-1980s

- Major interdiction efforts by the DEA and the U.S. Coast Guard effectively closed off Florida as a secure entry point for drug trafficking. This led the traffickers to choose a new route for entry into the United States, through Central America and Mexico.

1985

- February–March: DEA Special Agent Enrique Camarena was abducted, tortured, and murdered by five persons involved in the drug trade in Mexico. Camarena had reportedly uncovered a multibillion dollar drug scam in which he suspected officers of the Mexican policy forces, the army, and the government.
- February 17: The Camarena murder led to a second Operation Intercept, involving strict inspection of vehicles and then partial closing of the border.

1986

- April 8: President Ronald Reagan signs National Security Decision Directive No. 221, naming counternarcotics efforts as a national security issue. This called for a great role in the effort by U.S. military forces and the Central Intelligence Agency.
- August: Vice President George H. W. Bush launches Operation Alliance to coordinate interdiction activities among fifteen federal agencies and four state and local agencies with responsibilities along the U.S.-Mexico border. The intent was to coordinate activities with Mexican security forces, but this did not succeed because of Mexican sovereignty concerns.
- October 27: The Anti-Drug Abuse and Control Act is passed in the United States, providing six billion dollars in new funding over three

years for drug enforcement and interdiction efforts, education to stimulate demand reduction, and treatment programs. The law also required that foreign assistance be withheld from countries the president could not certify had cooperated fully with the United States or taken adequate steps on their own to prevent drug production and trafficking and drug-related money laundering.

1988

- The Mexican president Miguel de la Madrid, early in the year, declares drug trafficking to be a national security issue. This shifted much responsibility in antidrug efforts to the president's office.
- November 19: The U.S. Anti-Drug Abuse and Control Act of 1988 increased funding for antinarcotic activities. The act required that certified countries sign a treaty with the United States to cooperate with the U.S. Treasury Department to identify money-laundering activities.
- December 1: Carlos Salinas de Gortari takes the office as president of Mexico and promises greater antidrug cooperation with the United States in a "new era of friendship."
- December 20: The United Nations Convention Against Illicit Traffic in Narcotic Drugs and Psychotropic Substances is opened for signature. The United States and Mexico eventually sign.

1989

- January 20: President George H. W. Bush takes office. There is a quadrupling of spending for military involvement in drug control efforts at U.S. borders and elsewhere during his administration.
- October 4: Salinas, in an address to a joint session of the Mexican Congress, says that Mexico will cooperate with the United States on drug-control efforts, but that "there will be no joint military operations on our soil."

1990

- April: The U.S. DEA sponsors the kidnapping on Mexican soil of Humberto Álvarez Macháin, a doctor suspected of involvement in the torture and murder of Agent Camarena.
- June: The Mexican Northern Border Response Force began to test a cooperative interdiction program with the U.S. DEA and Defense Department. When the media discovers and publicizes that U.S. Customs aircraft patrolling the Pacific Ocean and the Caribbean will be allowed to overfly parts of Mexican airspace, Salinas quickly disbands the program.

- June: The U.S. Department of Justice reaches a provisional agreement with the Salinas government to permit Mexican police forces to operate in the United States on terms similar to those guiding DEA activities in Mexico. In return, Mexico grants diplomatic immunity to DEA agents in Mexico.

1992

- June 15: The U.S. Supreme Court holds in *United States v. Álvarez-Macháin* that "the fact of [a suspect's] forcible abduction does not prohibit his trial in a U.S. court for violations of this country's criminal laws." Álvarez-Macháin was eventually acquitted of the U.S. charges against him.

1995

- October: U.S. Secretary of Defense William Perry visits Mexico to discuss antidrug measures. This was the first time a sitting defense secretary had visited Mexico.

Late 1990s

- A series of allegations of corruption in Mexico's drug enforcement agencies during the administration of President Ernesto Zedillo undermine confidence in Mexico's efforts. The most notable case is that of General Jesús Gutierrez Rebello, the chief of Mexico's National Institute to Combat Drugs and formerly the commander of military zones with a heavy presence of drug traffickers in 1996. General Gutierrez Rebello was later convicted and sentenced to thirty-five years in prison for protecting the known drug lord Amado Carrillo in exchange for money and gifts.

1998

- June: A political fiasco erupts over a clandestine operation by U.S. law enforcement agencies code-named Operation Casablanca to crack down on money laundering in Mexico. The operation was apparently carried out without official Mexican knowledge. Zedillo later said that no country "is entitled to violate other countries' laws for the sake of enforcing its own."

2001

- October 24: The U.S. Senate passes a bill to end strict narcotics certification requirements for countries in the Western Hemisphere.

2005

- November: The Mexican Supreme Court reverses a 2001 ruling that prohibited the extradition of alleged criminals to another country if they faced life imprisonment. This ruling led to the extradition of sixty-three persons to the United States in 2006 alone.

2006

- April: Mexican President Vicente Fox vetoed a measure passed by the congress that would have decriminalized the holding of small amounts of drugs for personal use, allegedly under intense pressure from the United States.

2008

- June 30: U.S. President George W. Bush signs the Mérida Initiative law to provide $400 million in antidrug funding to Mexico, with some of these funds going to Central American countries, in U.S. fiscal year 2009. This appropriation is intended to be the first installment of a three-year antidrug program of $1.6 billion.

  The Mérida Initiative came about when Mexican President Felipe Calderón met with Bush in Mérida, Yucatan, in 2007 and suggested that the antidrug program in Mexico should involve more cooperation from the United States.

- November: Tony Garza, the U.S. ambassador to Mexico, in a speech in Texas, says that "Mexico would not be . . . experiencing this level of violence were the United States not the largest consumer of illicit drugs and the main supplier of weapons to the cartels."

2009

- February 11: The Latin American Commission on Drugs and Democracy—headed by the former presidents Fernando Henrique Cardoso of Brazil, César Gaviria of Colombia, and Ernesto Zedillo of Mexico—recommend the decriminalization of marijuana use.

- March 25: U.S. Secretary of State Hillary Clinton, during her first official visit to Mexico, says: "Our [the United States's] insatiable demand for illegal drugs fuels the drug trade. . . . Our inability to prevent weapons from being illegally smuggled across the border to arm these criminals causes the deaths of police officers, soldiers, and civilians." This was the first statement by an official of this high rank to publicly admit the U.S. role in Mexico's drug violence.

- April 19: U.S. President Barack Obama, at the Fifth Summit of the Americas in Port of Spain, Trinidad, announces his intention to seek U.S. ratification of the 1997 Inter-American Convention Against the Illicit Manufacturing and Trafficking in Firearms, Ammunition, Explosives, and Other Related Materials (CIFTA).

Energy
The Oil Is Ours

Pemex was the sixth most important petroleum producer in 2000, the ninth in 2004, the tenth in 2006, and the eleventh in 2007.
—MEXICAN SECRETARIAT OF ENERGY AND PETROLEOS MEXICANOS, 2007

Without private capital, expertise, and greater financial freedom for Pemex, it will be nearly impossible for Mexico to maintain its status as a major oil exporter.
—SARAH O. LADISLAW, 2008

Mexico's nationalist sentiment is more profound on oil than on any other issue. This nationalism has its ideological base in the expropriation of the assets of foreign oil companies under President Lázaro Cárdenas in 1938. The circumstances surrounding Cárdenas's action—the refusal of the oil companies to heed legal orders—added to the nationalistic fervor. The event is a part of Mexican history that all children learn about in school. The 1917 constitution states that Mexico has direct dominion over its natural resources—a major reason why the population gives special attention to government ownership of oil. This reality can be seen in the timeline of events at the end of the chapter.

Oil Nationalism

Mexico is one of the most restrictive countries in the world with respect to granting risk contracts, especially to foreign oil companies, in which the investor gets a share of the profits based on its contribution to oil discovery and production. National oil companies (NOCs) of China, Cuba, Russia, Venezuela, and even North Korea are prepared to enter into joint ventures with private foreign investors, both international oil companies and NOCs.[1] So are other NOCs in the Western Hemisphere.[2] Aramco of Saudi Arabia, like Mexico, currently does not enter into joint ventures with foreign companies. The fact that the oil in the ground or under the sea belongs to the home country is a standard situation throughout most of the world, but this has not prevented other countries from entering into joint ventures using risk contracts. It is unclear whether the Mexican public is aware of the degree of its own country's restrictiveness—or that it would matter if they were. The Mexican public, in poll after poll, consistently makes clear its opposition to allowing foreigners and even Mexican companies to have risk contracts in oil exploration and production.[3]

Mexico's ultranationalism on private and foreign investment in oil is particularly salient at this time. For example, production at Cantarell, Mexico's largest oil deposit, has been falling consistently since 2006—by about 25 percent, with little prospect of recovery.[4] Mexican crude production from all national oil sources peaked in 2004 at 3,383 thousand barrels a day, was down to 3,082 thousand barrels a day in 2007, and continued to fall in 2008.[5] In April through June of 2008, Pemex's oil exports fell by 11.5 percent compared with the same period in 2007, from 1.7 million to 1.4 million barrels a day. This affects U.S. oil supplies because about 80 percent of Mexico's oil exports typically go to the United States.[6] Mexico's proven reserves of crude have declined by 7.6 percent from 2003 to 2007 and are now estimated by Pemex at about 14 billion barrels.[7]

The current level of proven oil reserves—assuming that it is between, say, eleven billion and fourteen billion barrels—would not be a cause of deep concern if new discoveries approximately equal to domestic demand and exports were being found. But they are not. It is not possible to predict what Mexico's new oil finds will be, and it therefore follows that one cannot know how many years Mexico will be able to supply its domestic needs from its reserves. It is not possible to know the level of oil exports Mexico might be able to sustain in the years ahead. It *is* possible that Mexico will become an oil importer during the next decade. A question one hears from oil experts in Mexico is: Will Mexico make the necessary policy changes *before* it becomes an oil importer, or will the changes come only *after* the trauma of becoming an oil importer takes place? The United States became an oil importer in the 1960s, and there have been futile calls ever since for the country to become energy independent. There would likely be a similar reaction in Mexico if it became an oil importer.

Problems Facing Pemex

Pemex's problems are legion. Perhaps the most serious, however, is the large sums that are skimmed each year from Pemex's gross revenue to finance about 40 percent of Mexico's federal budget. There are two reasons why Pemex is used for this purpose: (1) it is already there, bringing money into Mexico; and (2) federal tax collections over many years have averaged only about 11 percent of gross domestic product, which is not enough to finance an expenditure budget that comes closer to 18 percent of GDP. One consequence of Treasury's skimming is that Pemex over the years has lacked the resources from its own income to engage in sufficient exploration. To deal with this problem, an alternative financing technique known as PIDIREGAS (Proyectos de Inversión Diferida en el Registro del Gasto, or long-term productive infrastructure projects) was devised to permit borrowing from the private sector until an infrastructure project is completed. These borrowings did not show up in public sector accounts until the private lenders were compensated from the proceeds of the completed project. At that time ownership of the project shifted to the public sector. This technique was used by other institutions in addition to Pemex for projects that generate a revenue stream. PIDIREGAS obligations are sovereign debt.[8] The technique is no longer being used by Pemex to fund new exploration and production.

One consequence of the taxing of Pemex beyond what normal royalties would be is that in most years Pemex operates at a loss—no matter what the price of oil is on the world market. The federal government sets a price for oil exports as a budgetary device, and in recent years (except for 2008, when market prices plummeted) this budgetary benchmark price has been lower than the price Mexican oil actually fetches.[9] This, in theory, gives the federal government some leeway in what it can provide to Pemex for exploration. This has been done to some extent, but much of this "excess," as it is called, has also been used for current expenditures, which creates its own problems.[10] Many of these points have been summarized by Adrián Lajous, a former head of Pemex who is now an energy consultant. He states that Pemex taxes and royalties are 62 percent of its sales and more than 110 percent of its gross revenues. The reserve/production ratio, according to Lajous, is less than ten years.[11]

If Mexico were able to increase its tax take, this theoretically could enable the government to finance more of the federal budget than is now the case. In turn, this theoretically should reduce the tax and royalty burden placed on Pemex. The word "theoretically" is used because, as seen in the way the government has been using the excess revenue from higher oil prices, this has just increased the level of current expenditures. In any event President Calderón did succeed in imposing new taxes designed to increase the tax take by one to two percentage points of GDP. This increase was made possible, in part, by indicating that the burden on Pemex would be reduced. It remains to be seen whether this will actually take place. The nature of the tax increase is described in chapter 1.

The labor union that represents the workers at Pemex (the Sindicato de Trabajadores Petroleros de la República Mexicana) is one of the strongest and most influential in Mexico. The union has much control over the hiring and firing of employees. It also has five members on the eleven-member adminis-trative council of Pemex. The 2008 Pemex legislation calls for four new board members who are referred to as "professional advisors." Pemex has more em-ployees in terms of its sales than any other large oil company; the exact num-ber varies from year to year, but the figure for mid-2008 was 141,000 for $103 billion of sales. In contrast, the Brazilian NOC Petróleo Brasileiro (Petrobras) had 69,000 employees for sales of $87 billion, and the ExxonMobil employee figure was 107,000 employees with sales of $372 billion.[12] Put another way, Pemex may be the least efficient large oil company in the world. Put in con-text, Pemex has a monopoly in Mexico on oil exploration, production, and marketing—it is the largest company of any kind in Mexico.

Pemex also lacks the technical capacity for drilling in deep waters. This is not because it lacks skilled personnel, but rather because the company's engineers and geologists have had no experience in deepwater drilling. The evidence is powerful that the prospects of finding large deposits of oil and natural gas in the deep waters of the Gulf of Mexico are more promising than in shallower waters and underground, where Pemex is now drilling for oil. Deepwater drilling is expensive, and unless every exploration is successful at hundreds of thousands of dollars for each try, Pemex lacks the resources to undertake these expensive searches. Mexican policy instead has been to offer service contracts for deepwater exploration for oil and gas. This is essentially an offer to hire foreign companies to do work for which they would be paid a service fee and perhaps a bonus if the exploration is successful.

Most big oil producers are not interested, however; they are not for hire but want risk contracts under which they would bear the cost if the exploration is unsuccessful and get the reward if the risk pays off. Petrobras, which has ample experience in deepwater drilling, was one of the companies that said it was not interested in working in Mexico as a service company.[13] Large oil companies also wish to record increases in oil reserves with the Securities and Exchange Commission of the United States because this enables them to borrow on the basis of these reserves. Mexican service contracts do not permit independent oil companies to record any reserves. If one looks at a map of the Gulf of Mexico that shows the location of oil and gas drilling, the U.S. side has been explored to the hilt, with much success, and the Mexican side is almost devoid of drilling except near the coastline at lower depths.[14]

A comparison of Mexican and Brazilian energy policies reveals many contrasts. Brazil in the 1970s started its experiments to produce ethanol using sugar cane. The large early subsidies became unnecessary when oil prices soared into the atmosphere, making sugar-based ethanol economical without subsidies. Today, Brazil is the world's second-largest ethanol producer, after the United States, and sugar cane is a more efficient biofuel base than corn, which the United States uses. Ethanol now constitutes about 40 percent of Brazilian vehicle fuel.[15] Mexico has little experience with converting its excess sugar production into ethanol.

Petrobras is an NOC, just as Pemex is, but it has two classes of stock: one voting and the other nonvoting. The Brazilian government has a majority of the voting shares, and private investors have a majority of the nonvoting shares. This structure, which was created in the early 1990s, has worked to keep Petrobras policy in the hands of the government and to force the company to seek to maximize its profits for the shareholders' benefit. Petrobras, during the past few years, has made some spectacular oil and natural gas discoveries in very deep waters off of Brazil's coast. Tupi, in the Santos Basin, for example, apparently contains five billion to seven billion barrels of oil in the presalt layer some 7,000 feet (2,140 meters) below the water's surface. Jupiter reportedly contains enough natural gas to make Brazil self-sufficient in about ten years. Carioca is a large oil pool, of which Tupi is a part, that apparently has some multiples of the Tupi find. All these discoveries come from joint ventures between Petrobras and foreign companies, with Petrobras holding the majority. It will take time and considerable money to bring these finds to market, though, and when that is done, Brazil will likely be a more important player in the world oil market than Mexico. Pragmatism has dominated Brazilian oil policy, whereas ideology has been dominant in Mexican oil policy.

President Calderón made a number of proposals in the spring of 2008 to make Pemex a more efficient company. His suggestions did not include amending the constitution to permit joint ventures with private companies in the exploration and production of oil. It did, however, discuss giving Pemex more flexibility in concluding service contracts with third parties. Other important changes in the president's proposal were: (1) add four professional advisers to Pemex's administrative council, two full-time and two part-time; (2) encourage the formation of technical committees of which two would be mandatory (on transparency and investment strategy); (3) give Pemex a new legal framework and more autonomy on its budgeting; and (4) encourage the sale of interest-bearing citizen bonds to bring the Mexican public closer to Pemex without giving the bondholders policy rights.[16] The bond sale idea reflects the Brazilian model (although the public inside and outside Brazil can buy shares in the company on many stock markets) and could have some significance in the future. The president also noted that Mexico must now refine much of its oil in foreign countries (in the United States), and he proposed that Pemex be given explicit authority to contract with private Mexican firms for the construction of future refineries in Mexico.

Because oil policy is a sensitive issue in Mexico, Calderón's proposals stimulated fierce political opposition. The president was forced to agree to a long period of debate that went on for many months. The PRI made a series of suggestions. One was that Pemex should establish new affiliates for construction of refineries and storage and transport of oil and oil products, and another was that the Mexican senate should have the right to ratify or veto senior professional appointments. The then head of Pemex, Jesús Reyes Heroles, who has long been a staunch supporter of the PRI, rejected the first suggestion because it would involve unnecessary spending that Pemex could not afford. He rejected the second idea because it would further politicize Pemex.[17]

The leading figure of the PRD, the man who barely lost the presidential election to Calderón in 2006, Andrés Manuel López Obrador, labeled the president's proposals as the "privatization" of Pemex. It is hard to justify this categorization, however, other than to use a loaded word to arouse public sentiment against the president's submission. The PRD, the most leftist of Mexico's three main parties, did suggest that union representation on Pemex's administrative council be reduced from five to one. The PRI favored keeping the five union members on this council; so did Calderón's proposal. Mexico's top business group, the Consejo Coordinador Empresarial, later endorsed the PRD position regarding one union representative on a smaller administrative council. Most of the president's proposal was eventually enacted into law. The problem of declining oil production hardly came up in the energy debate. Perhaps the most lucid comment on the different party positions was in an op-ed column in *Reforma* by Luis Rubio, a respected political analyst. His point was that Pemex is a sacred cow in Mexico, the oil union is a sacred cow, and everything that some groups do not wish to change also becomes sacred, which annuls discussion or analysis.[18]

U.S. Energy Problems

The United States has about 5 percent of the world's population and consumes upward of 20 percent of the world's oil.[19] In the first half of 2008 there was a drop of 800,000 barrels per day in U.S. oil demand from what it had been in 2007. The U.S. Energy Information Administration (EIA) attributed this to slow U.S. economic growth in 2008 and high oil prices in the early part of the year. The demand for oil is price inelastic, but not completely so. The higher oil and natural gas prices of recent years have encouraged U.S. companies to use energy more efficiently. The EIA estimate is that U.S. oil use in 2009 will be 20.8 million barrels per day. Oil is used primarily in this country for transportation. The United States has been an oil importer since the late 1960s. Figure 5.1 shows the most recent sources for U.S. oil imports.

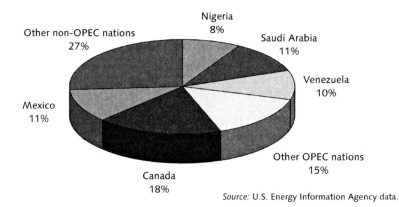

Source: U.S. Energy Information Agency data.

Figure 5.1. Sources of U.S. oil imports in 2007 (percent)

Coal, because it is relatively cheap and abundant in the United States, is used to generate about half of U.S. electricity. Coal emits high levels of carbon dioxide, however, which contributes heavily to global warming. It is near impossible in the medium term to find cleaner replacements for coal to generate electricity (figure 5.2); consequently, the official corrective—and the solution advocated by President Obama—is to rely on technology to make coal "clean." This has not been well spelled out by the administration, nor is it a central part of the public discourse. The best known way to make coal use clean is to sequestrate and then store the carbon dioxide, but the cost of doing this could be enormous and the technology is not yet fully developed.

The U.S. energy situation has been studied meticulously inside and outside the government.[20] The discussion here focuses on what are seen as U.S. policy shortcomings as a counterpoint to the earlier discussion on Mexico and its "sacred cows." Regarding the United States and energy, we touch on the same theme by referring to the power of special interests. In both cases the central problem is the failure of the political system to maximize efficiency in energy policy. U.S. politicians have repeatedly advocated "energy independence" since the United States has become an oil importer. A study on the national security implications of oil dependency issued in 2006 by a special task force for the Council on Foreign Relations listed the goal of energy independence as "Myth Number One."[21] This goal can be described merely as a political ploy to attract public attention, but it has had adverse policy consequences.

The subsidies granted by the U.S. government for the production of corn-based ethanol, coupled with the high protective barriers imposed on imports

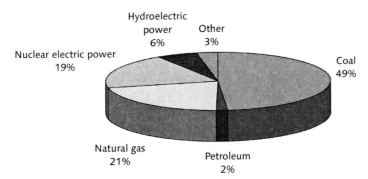

Source: U.S. Energy Information Agency data.

Figure 5.2. Methods of U.S. electricity generation in 2007 (percent)

of higher quality, more efficient sugar-based ethanol produced in Brazil, can be justified only by the specious argument that this policy contributes to energy independence in the United States.[22] U.S. security would surely be enhanced if global ethanol production using a sugar or cellulosic base were encouraged via duty-free entry into the United States. The use of cellulosic materials to produce ethanol would also remove the push given to higher food and feed prices for corn to which U.S. ethanol policy contributes.

In the face of lobbying for the status quo by U.S. automobile manufacturers, the United States was slow to raise the corporate average fuel economy standard. The lobbying was understandable in light of the loss of market to foreign brands, but this adamancy against adapting to changed competitive circumstances was an important cause of financial losses by U.S. companies and their need for a bailout by the U.S. government in early 2009. After much delay, these changes by U.S. producers are now taking place. The U.S. Congress was slow to provide appropriations for better public transportation, even after it was clear that the demand for oil by large emerging market countries like China and India was growing rapidly. Before Barack Obama became president, the United States did not join most of the rest of the world in policies to reduce global warming, despite the evidence that this would cost more the longer it was delayed. Martin Wolf of the *Financial Times* has dealt succinctly with this issue: "Fundamental innovation and high prices on greenhouse gas emissions must follow."[23] Obama's energy proposals take into account the need to reduce greenhouse gases that engender global warming.

The U.S. Congress has been ambivalent about whether it wants more oil imports from Canada, the number-one foreign supplier of oil to the United States, or whether its priority is on environmental protection. Like Yogi Berra, who said that "when you come to a fork in the road, take it," the Congress has chosen both—more oil and more environmental protection, the first for the large quantity of oil imports from Canada and the second for the less abundant governmental imports. Most of the oil that Canada ships to the United States comes from its Athabasca oil sands and is considered unconventional oil. Getting oil from Canada's oil sands is highly polluting; it uses and pollutes enormous quantities of water, has high greenhouse gas emissions, and requires much burning of natural gas, an expensive input.[24] Section 526 of the most recent U.S. energy legislation prohibits the import of synthetic fuel whose emissions are higher than from the use of conventional fuel.[25]

It has become evident that the United States must use renewable energy sources more extensively as it becomes serious about reducing the emission of greenhouse gases while still generating enough electricity for domestic users. There is much sentiment in favor of building more nuclear energy facilities, and this may come to pass despite the high up-front expenditures and the unsolved problem of storing the nuclear waste. Large-scale solar- and wind-power facilities are likely to play a much larger role in future electricity generation. Natural gas is becoming more abundant in the United States and may replace coal to some extent in electricity generation. The most important requirement for meeting the twin objectives of increasing power generation and reducing the current level of environmental degradation may be technological innovation.

The United States, from time to time, raises the issue of greater energy solidarity among the countries of the Western Hemisphere. This cooperation exists between the United States and Canada, and to a lesser degree between these two and Mexico, but is not the case in the rest of the hemisphere. Eduardo Gudynas, the director of the Latin American Center of Social Ecology in Montevideo, Uruguay, has described this well: "Energy integration, in the sense of having common energy resources, elaborating joint undertakings, and helping shared productive initiatives, does not exist."[26] The Western Hemisphere supplies about half of U.S. oil imports, and as Mexican supplies become more uncertain, Brazilian oil resources are increasing.

Mexico-U.S. Energy Interaction

Adrián Lajous, writing about Mexico's foreign petroleum policy before the election that brought Felipe Calderón into the presidency, listed five tasks that the new president would have to confront: (1) the decline in Mexico's oil production, which started in 1995; (2) the prolonged fall in Mexico's oil reserves; (3) the fact that Mexico has become a substantial importer of petroleum products; (4) passage of the dominance in the oil market to the sellers; and (5) the growing concerns of oil and natural gas consumers about security of supply.[27] He concluded that Mexico would have to give priority to domestic supplies as a matter of national security, and this would require a decline in exports. It is evident that Mexican oil production is declining. This is a significant reality for the United States because Mexico has been the second-largest oil exporter to the United States for many years. Lajous also noted that the United States, for both security and economic reasons, prefers to import oil from nearby countries. This will continue to be possible from Canada as long as oil sands production keeps growing, and probably from Venezuela, although its president, Hugo Chávez, would like to shift more of his country's oil exports to China. Brazil may one day be able to ship meaningful quantities of oil to the United States, but that will take at least ten years. Lajous's advice to an incoming Mexican president is just as apt for the new U.S. president, in that he must look to other sources of U.S. oil supplies now that Mexico is unlikely to be a reliable future supplier.

In the debate on President Calderón's proposal for changing the structure of Pemex, the PRI congressional delegation proposed that a Pemex affiliate should be created to build more oil refineries in Mexico. That may not be the top priority in Mexico's energy expenditures because if oil production is inadequate, new refinery capacity will have to use foreign oil to produce gasoline and diesel. This would mean importing more crude oil and fewer oil products, but at a high cost in refinery construction. Mexico now imports significant quantities of petroleum products. Half of the gasoline used in Mexico today is imported and that proportion will probably increase in future years. "We will do what we must do," is the way the director of Pemex put it.[28] The increased imports are attributed to Mexico's larger vehicle fleet and a reduced rhythm of production by Mexico's refineries.

This is part of a bigger picture of Mexico-U.S. interaction on Mexico's oil product imports. Mexico in the past subsidized the prices of petroleum and electricity, and the cost was about twenty billion dollars in 2008.[29] This is a populist policy, but hardly an economic proposition in that Mexico was paying more to buy gasoline in the United States than it charged at Pemex gasoline pumps. To add insult to economic injury, Americans who live at the border crossed into Mexico to buy gasoline and diesel at the cheaper Mexican prices. Mexico's energy minister, Georgina Kessel, announced that the prices of gasoline and diesel would be raised gradually to bring them up to U.S. prices, and that has taken place to a great extent. This puts pressure on Mexico's inflation rate, and there were rumblings in early 2009 that gasoline prices would be lowered again.

U.S.-Mexico Energy Tension

Full agreement on energy issues between the United States and Mexico has not existed since the expropriation of the assets of U.S. and other foreign oil companies in 1938. One can go back even further to the Mexican Constitution of 1917. The fact that Mexico claims ownership of the oil under its ground and under the sea within its maritime limits is not the central problem, despite the slogan one hears frequently: "The Oil Is Ours." So is the oil in Brazil, Canada, Norway, and other countries. Neither is the problem the existence of a national oil company; Brazil, Norway, Saudi Arabia, Venezuela, and most other countries also have NOCs. The tension is not caused by Pemex's relative inefficiency, such as its overstaffing; this penalizes Mexico economically, but companies have generally learned to deal with inefficient counterparts. One can even argue that Mexico's rigid restrictions on allowing risk ventures with private companies, foreign and domestic, would not be the problem that it is if Pemex had been more successful in finding new sources of oil. Had Mexico over the years been able to collect more taxes to fund the federal budget, Pemex might have been able to operate as a normal oil company rather than being used as a cash cow to fill the central budget gap. If Mexico becomes a net oil importer, the government may have to make an impossible choice—either give up taxing Pemex to finance the government's budget, or raise overall tax collections. The latter may be just as hard to accomplish.

Mexico's oil policy can be considered a perfect storm: Mexico has rigid restrictions on private equity investment; this is coupled with the skimming of more than 100 percent of Pemex's gross revenue, thereby limiting its exploration activities; the country has an exceedingly low level of tax collection in relation to GDP; and Pemex has been politicized more than most other NOCs, as is evident from the size of its staff relative to the value of output. At the heart of the tension is a contentious bilateral situation: the United States needs to import increasingly larger quantities of oil, and Mexico, as a result of its policies, is becoming an insecure supplier. The recent energy debate in Mexico stimulated by Calderón's proposals on changes in Pemex did not directly address how Mexico could make itself into a more secure supplier of oil, either for itself or for export.

The history of Mexican-U.S. hydrocarbon relations fits the pattern of the other sectoral issues discussed in this book, a defensive posture on the Mexican side and a more aggressive one the U.S. side because of the need for imports. There were lengthy discussions during the 1970s when Mexico still had a surplus of natural gas on how some of this gas would be sold to the United States, and at what price. In the end agreement eluded the negotiators on the issue of price. The then Mexican president José López Portillo was livid with

anger at the breakdown and accused the United States of bad faith. The sentiment in the U.S. government was that Mexico was pricing its gas too high,
especially in light of the lower price then being paid by the United States for
Canadian natural gas.[30]

NAFTA and its aftermath brought the United States and Mexico a bit closer on oil issues, but not by very much. In a well-researched article, the economist Antonio Ortiz Mena has described how Mexico was able to achieve its
key goals in negotiating NAFTA even though it said "no" five times on energy: (1) "no" to foreign investment in oil exploration, production, and refining in Mexico; (2) "no" to risk-sharing contracts with payment in oil reserves;
(3) "no" to energy supply commitments; (4) "no" gas imports other than
through Pemex; and (5) "no" foreign retail outlets.[31] The title of the article,
"Getting to 'No,'" asserts that Mexico was defending itself against U.S. energy
demands. In 2001, NAFTA spawned the North American Energy Working
Group (NAEWG), which has issued some valuable reports agreed to jointly
by experts from all three NAFTA countries.

Despite its positive contributions to the work of the NAEWG, however, Mexico is unable to be a full-fledged partner on North American energy issues.
Mexico is no longer confident that it can produce enough oil to meet even
its own needs. It does not produce enough natural gas to meet its needs, nor
does it refine enough gasoline and diesel to meet its own consumption. One
area in which Mexican energy cooperation will be beneficial to the United
States is the construction of regasification facilities on Mexico's western coast
to receive liquefied natural gas for its own and U.S. use.

There is no reason for Mexico to privatize Pemex as such, any more than
the policy aspects of Petrobras have been privatized, and President Calderón
promised in his recent proposal that this would not be done. Privatization of
oil, however, has a unique meaning in Mexico, one that does not apply to the
rest of the world. In most other countries joint ventures between NOCs and
private companies are not taboo; in Mexico, though, this would be considered
privatization. This historic and ideological position is important to Mexicans
and has been built into their collective psyche. Mexico's oil ideology as such
should not be important to the United States; what *is* important to the United
States is more mundane—namely, to have a reliable supplier of oil regardless
of the ideology of who produces it. These different outlooks—ideology with
diminishing Mexican oil production versus U.S. pragmatism and the uncer-

tainty that Mexico will be a reliable oil supplier—are now creating considerable tension in Mexico-U.S. energy relations.

Energy: The Oil Is Ours

1917
- Article 27 of the Mexico Constitution of 1917 gives the nation direct
  dominion over the country's natural resources.

1938
- March 18: President Lázaro Cárdenas expropriates the facilities of foreign oil companies.
- June 7: Cárdenas issues an official decree creating Petróleos Mexicanos
  (Pemex), giving it exclusive rights over exploration, production, and
  commercialization of oil in Mexico. Pemex begins operations on June
  20.

1945
- January 15: A decree is published in the *Diario oficial* promulgating the
  compensation for the expropriation of the assets of the U.S. oil companies. The agreed sum was just under twenty-eight million dollars.

1949
- January 11: A decree is published in the *Diario oficial* establishing the
  operating responsibilities of the Federal Electricity Commission (the
  Comisión Federal de Electricidad, CFE).

1958
- November 29: The Petroleum Act of 1958 defines the scope of Article 27
  of the Mexican constitution.

Late 1960s
- The United States becomes a net importer of oil.

1977
- August 4: The U.S. Department of Energy is established during President
  Jimmy Carter's administration.
- August–December: Controversy over the price of Mexican natural gas
  sales to the United States via pipeline leads to Mexican cancellation of
  the proposed project.

1978
- May: The United States begins to buy crude oil from Pemex for the U.S.
  Strategic National Reserve that had been established in 1975.

1992

- July 16: The Organic Law of Pemex and Subsidiary Bodies (the Ley Orgánica de Petróleos Mexicanos y Organismos Subsidiarios) calls for dividing Pemex into four independent operating divisions: (1) exploration and production, (2) natural gas and basic petrochemicals, (3) refining, and (4) secondary petrochemicals.

1994

- January 1: NAFTA goes into effect, but Mexico made few concessions during the negotiation of chapter 6 on energy. In effect, NAFTA consists of two separate agreements on energy: one between the United States and Canada in which cooperation is extensive, and one between the United States and Mexico in which cooperation is limited.

1995

- October 31: The Law of the Energy Regulatory Commission (the Ley de la Comisión Reguladora de Energía), establishing the commission, is published in the *Diario oficial.*

1999

- February: President Ernesto Zedillo sends a proposal to the Mexican congress requesting a constitutional change to allow privatization of the country's electricity sector. The inability to get the necessary two-thirds vote forced Zedillo to withdraw his plan a year later.

2001

- April 22: At the conclusion of a Summit of the Americas meeting, Presidents Vicente Fox and George Bush along with Prime Minister Jean Chrétien agree to establish a North American Energy Working Group (NAEWG).

2003

- May 8: Mexico's Energy Regulatory Commission grants its first permit to allow a foreign corporation to build a regasification plant. The plant will receive liquefied natural gas on the western coast of Mexico to serve both Mexico and the United States.

2005

- March 23: Presidents Fox and Bush and Prime Minister Stephen Martin sign the Security and Prosperity Partnership (SPP) agreement to promote North American integration, including in the energy sector.

2007

- January 17: The U.S. National Petroleum Council releases a study, "Facing the Hard Truths about Energy: A Comprehensive View to 2030 of Oil and Natural Gas," which provides accurate energy data to the interested public.
- November 28: Mexico releases an energy policy program for 2007–2012.

2008

- April 8: Calderón proposes legislation, the main goal of which is to modernize Pemex. The proposal arouses considerable controversy and at least seventy-one days are set aside for debate, congressional hearings, and to hear opinions of Mexican worthies. The proposal contains nothing regarding constitutional change, but many opponents of the president charge that it is "privatization" because it calls for service contracts for exploring in the deep waters of the Gulf of Mexico, where the prospects for finding oil and natural gas deposits are favorable. The proposal contemplates bonuses for the companies that find oil and gas. Most of Calderón's proposals are ultimately enacted into law.
- July: Mexico's minister of energy discloses that Mexico has been in discussion since January with private oil companies exploring for oil and natural gas in deep waters on the U.S. side of the Gulf of Mexico. These explorations are close to Mexican waters, and the discussions relate to what benefits Mexico would receive if there are findings in what may be considered transnational waters. Mexico is not drilling in its own deep waters of the Gulf.

2009

- March 20: Pemex issues a report that provides data on hydrocarbon reserves as of January 1, 2009. The figure for proven reserves of oil was 14.3 billion barrels, 409 billion barrels fewer than a year earlier.

Migration
A Consequence of Inequality

Effective [U.S.] immigration policy must contain a comprehensive mix of measures, including stronger border controls and internal enforcement processes.
—RAY MARSHALL, 2007

He [U.S. President Barack Obama] should return to the approach followed by all of his predecessors until 2006: stop illegal entrants at the border when possible, but refrain from hunting them down once they cross the border.
—JORGE G. CASTAÑEDA, 2008

The estimate of the U.S. Census Bureau is that there are about twelve million people in the United States who were born in Mexico. This represents a fifteen-fold increase since 1970.[1] The Mexican-born population in the United States now amounts to more than 10 percent of the Mexican population in Mexico. Among developed countries of the Organization for Economic Cooperation and Development, the United States is truly an immigration country—with immigrants not only from Mexico. In 2005 more than thirty-eight million foreign-born, about 13 percent of the total population, lived in the United States. In absolute numbers Germany was second after the United States, with 10.6 million foreign-born people living there.[2]

A statistic that has deep implications for both the United States and Mexico is that between 2002 and the first part of 2008, more Mexicans found jobs in the United States than they did in formal employment in Mexico—2.37 million compared with 2.21 million.[3] This reflects a situation that was not supposed to happen after Mexico and the United States entered into free trade with NAFTA—namely, that the U.S. GDP would grow at a higher *rate* than Mexico's. Francisco Alba, a respected Mexican economic-demographic scholar, has pointed out that from 1982 (when Mexico experienced a debt crisis and economic downturn) to 2006 per capita GDP in Mexico grew by only 0.5 percent a year. There was no movement toward economic convergence between Mexico and the United States; indeed, there was further divergence.[4] The model that economic integration proponents had in mind for NAFTA was what happened in Spain and Ireland after the two countries became part of what is now the European Union—their economies grew faster for many years than those of the more advanced countries.[5] Mexico's per capita income does not have to be equal to that of the United States to dampen the push to emigrate; however, it is necessary for parents to have confidence that good jobs exist at home for themselves and their children. That confidence does not now exist. The reasons for the failure of more robust economic growth in Mexico after NAFTA are discussed in chapters 1 and 2.

Since 1997, Mexico has had divided government, with the president facing a congressional majority from other political parties. President Felipe Calderón is a member of the PAN and the other two large parties, the PRI and the PRD, together hold more seats than the PAN in the legislature. The congress and the president have not been able to fully come together on basic structural reforms on fiscal issues, taxes, labor laws, energy, education, monopolies, infrastructure, and regulatory modernization.[6] Each political party protects its sacred cows and, consequently, economic growth is lagging. Calderón has been trying to make progress on many of these issues, with modest success, but hardly enough to overcome the underlying problems. Taking action against the home-grown impediments to Mexican economic growth is the only durable way to slow the pressures to emigrate. Calderón has made this point repeatedly.

The one imperative for adequate job-creation, in Mexico and elsewhere, is a reasonably high rate of economic growth and, as Alba pointed out, Mexico has not achieved this since the early 1980s. To create enough jobs for those entering the labor force, Mexico needs overall real growth in GDP of about 6 to 7 percent a year, or about 5 percent per capita—and it has been getting about 2.5 percent growth in overall GDP and about half of 1 percent a year on a per capita basis. This swells the ranks of the informal economy and pushes energetic Mexicans to cross the border, where they can earn seven to eight times more than at home.[7] A high rate of economic growth is necessary to reduce poverty in Mexico; the evidence for this is universal as long as the desire to reduce poverty is part of government policy. None of this argues that U.S. immigration policy is optimal, however—it is not. Nor does it imply that U.S. financial assistance to Mexico should be withheld.

Mexican Migration Policy

For many years Mexico had a policy to have no policy on migration to the United States. As stated in the 1998 *Binational Study* of the two countries, "Mexico . . . stayed aloof from the debate on changes in U.S. immigration policy, and this political stance undoubtedly was optimal for meeting Mexico's interests over many years."[8] The development that convinced Mexico to change its policy was the immigration debate in the United States involving the Hesburgh Commission in the late 1970s and culminating in the passage of the Immigration Reform and Control Act of 1986 (IRCA). An early example of the change from "no policy" to active engagement with the United States on migration policy was the Mexican initiative to have the *Binational Study* and to support the ground rules that the researchers from the two countries should agree on their conclusions in five main issue areas examined.[9] Perhaps the outstanding example of a direct Mexican effort to influence U.S. immigration legislation was Jorge Castañeda's call for the "whole enchilada" when he was the Mexican foreign minister.

If energetic young Mexicans of both sexes are unable to find satisfactory jobs at home, the ability to emigrate clearly serves as an escape valve that reduces internal tensions. For many years Mexicans who stayed home looked down on their compatriots in the United States; the reason for this probably had much to do with nationalism that Mexicans in Mexico are allegedly more patriotic than Mexicans who have left to live in the United States. It is in the same category as the expression used in Mexico to castigate those who support giving economic concessions to Americans and other foreigners; the word *vendepatrias*, meaning "selling the country," is heard often in Mexican political speeches. After 1982, when economic development from within collapsed and export promotion and seeking to maximize foreign direct investment (FDI) became hallmarks of development policy, the Mexican authorities realized that their expatriate communities could be assets. They were given concessions, such as dual nationality and the right to vote, and they were organized with government help.

The ability to find work opportunities abroad not only reduced internal tensions, but the large remittances from expatriate Mexicans, both legal residents and those without papers, are substantial—they were estimated to be twenty-four billion dollars in 2007 but declined by more than 3 percent in 2008 and are declining further in 2009.[10] The decline is the result of lower U.S. economic growth, higher food prices, and the decline in U.S. construction. Mexico's remittance receipts generally exceed FDI inflows.

Mexican authorities never say explicitly that emigration is an escape valve, but their behavior makes this evident. The argument instead is that the two economies are complementary, that Mexican labor helps U.S. agriculture, construction, and such low-skill service activities as working in hotels and restaurants. Mexican leaders and scholars also make the point that migration is a natural phenomenon. The solution to the emigration policy that President Calderón espouses whenever he can is greater economic growth in Mexico. Each of these arguments has validity, but the impression one gets is that Mexico hopes to delay drastic anti-immigrant action in the United States until a friendlier (that is, Democratic) Congress is elected, as happened in November 2008. There is fear that the strong measures being taken to find, arrest, often imprison, and then deport unauthorized immigrants in the United States would augment instability in Mexico. There is also concern in Mexico about separating families when undocumented immigrants are arrested during raids on industrial plants because family members are often U.S.-born spouses and children. Family separation can be ended if the Obama administration and Congress are able to enact a path toward legalization for the roughly six million to seven million Mexicans now living without documents in the United States. Getting such legislation does not have a high priority for 2009, but apparently it is on the Obama agenda for 2010.

Seeking delay in U.S. action against undocumented immigrants was an understandable posture on Mexico's part. The escape-valve aspect is a sign of dependency, at least until the pressure to leave Mexico is ended by economic growth, and that may be a long time in coming. Mexico also hopes—probably *expects* when the U.S. economy recovers—that the United States will institute a large temporary worker program that would authorize legal entry for hundreds of thousand of Mexicans into the United States. Mexico has its own problems on its southern border, as numerous Central Americans enter without documents. Some remain in Mexico and many others use Mexico as a route to the United States. Entering Mexico without documents has been a criminal offense, but this was changed in April 2008 to a civil offense that could be covered with a fine. The argument used to bring about the change was to regularize these unauthorized immigrants and to respect their human rights.[11]

U.S. Immigration Policy

According to the Pew Hispanic Center, Mexicans constitute between 50 percent and 60 percent of the estimated twelve million undocumented foreigners in the United States. Most of them crossed clandestinely into the United States on foot, hidden in cars and trucks, and sometimes on boats. Most of the remaining unauthorized immigrants are other Latin Americans, many of whom who entered the United States through Mexico. Still other immigrants entered the United States with valid visas but then overstayed their allowed time; they are referred to as "overstayers." There surely are Mexicans, other Latin Americans, and Caribbeans among the overstayers, but this group is made up largely of Asians, Canadians, Europeans, and others; they are generally more educated and have higher incomes than the clandestine border crossers. Most attention and resources have been devoted to preventing the undocumented entry of border crossers coming into the United States from Mexico.[12]

There are deep divisions in the United States about how to deal with Mexicans and other foreigners in the country without authorization. Many proposals from 2001 to 2007 never made it to a congressional vote (see the timeline at the end of the chapter), often because of the inability to invoke cloture against filibusters in the Senate. These include the DREAM Act, the AgJOBS Act, the REAL ID Act, the Kennedy-McCain Act, the Cornyn-Kyl bill that never made it out of committee, the Sensenbrenner bill that would have made unauthorized entry into the United States a criminal offense, and the proposal of Senate Majority Leader Harry Reid (D-Nevada) to provide a path toward legalization of undocumented immigrants. The differences on immigration legislation cut across party lines, encompassing the conservative wing of the Republican Party (these legislators oppose "amnesty") and the pro–labor union Democrats (who were prepared to legalize undocumented workers already in the country so that they could more easily be unionized, but did not want new entrants). It became clear in the final years of President George W. Bush's tenure that immigration legislation would have to wait at least until the next administration.

One aspect of the U.S. immigration debate—especially in its treatment of undocumented border crossers—is how mean-spirited this debate has become.[13] Some examples supporting this judgment are the following:

- The Congress in enacting IRCA refused to recommend a foolproof way of identifying whether job applicants were legally in the United States and chose as acceptable the kinds of documents that the experts warned could be easily forged. This gave employers an escape from being penalized for "knowingly" hiring undocumented workers. This was an implicit invitation for workers to enter the United States and use forged papers to get their jobs. Their crime, in essence, was to accept an invitation to come and work in the United States, papers or no papers.

- Employers hired labor contractors to find workers for them. This gave the employers deniability about knowing whether workers they employed were legitimately in the United States.

- After failing for more than fifteen years to even try to punish employers who knowingly hired unauthorized immigrants, the Department of Homeland Security took to raiding establishments where there is strong evidence that many unauthorized aliens work. When they find such workers, they are arrested, incarcerated, and then deported.

- In one infamous case a raid of this type on May 12, 2008, on a meat-processing plant in Pottsville, Iowa, led to the detention of hundreds of unauthorized immigrants, mostly from Guatemala, who were detained, shackled, and convinced to plead guilty to criminal charges for which 270 were sentenced to five months in prison instead of a possible felony penalty of two years for identity theft. After their imprisonment they were deported. Arrest, convince foreigners with little education and no English to reach a plea agreement, convict, imprison, deport—the purpose obviously was to send a message to others who accepted job offers implicitly made by U.S. employers.[14]

- On May 4, 2009, the U.S. Supreme Court rejected the use of aggravated identity theft unless the prosecution could show that the workers knew in advance that the fake Social Security numbers they used belonged to real persons.

- During a press conference, when asked about separating hundreds of thousands of U.S.-citizen children from their undocumented immigrant parents who are arrested and deported, Michael Chertoff, then secretary of Homeland Security, answered that "we can't allow the fact that someone who has a child who is an American citizen to create a de facto immunity from the law."[15] This, despite the fact that employers had been given de facto immunity from the law for many years.

In light of these problems, it is useful to ask some "what if" questions. What would the U.S. picture regarding the employment of unauthorized immigrants have been if employer penalties were imposed right after they were authorized when IRCA was passed in 1986? These penalties would have been meaningful if there was an effective way for employers to check on the bona fides of job applicants, and if the penalties were high enough to nullify the financial benefits of hiring low-paid illegal immigrants. The use of foolproof identity cards is controversial in the United States and other techniques for spotting illegality have been examined; these usually work through discrepancies in social security records. The reality as this is written is that there is no foolproof way to check whether prospective foreign workers are legally in the United States.

Foreigners who considered coming to work in the United States without authorization were informed through their networks that they would be welcomed by U.S. employers if they made it across the border during the years of little to no employer penalties. Similarly, they would have learned quickly through the grapevine, probably within days, which employers would be reluctant to hire them if employer penalties were significant. What would the size of unauthorized migration to the United States have been if the U.S. Congress and administration had been sincere about meaningful employer penalties? Based on U.S. Census data, some 10.3 million immigrants came to the United States between 2000 and 2007, the highest seven-year period in U.S. history. During peak years about five hundred thousand unauthorized Mexicans came to the United States each year to work.[16]

If work opportunities had been drastically reduced by effective employer penalties, it is doubtful that five hundred thousand unauthorized Mexicans would have paid the high *coyote* costs (*coyotes* are people who guide unauthorized Mexicans across the border for a fee) and risked an arduous journey that could cost an illegal border crosser his or her life. With the increase in U.S. Border Patrol agents along the Mexican border, coupled with increasingly sophisticated detection technology, the use of relatively easy routes across the border, especially into California and to a lesser extent into Texas, Mexican migrants were forced to use more treacherous routes to enter the United States. As a consequence, there have been more than four hundred deaths a year of Mexicans seeking to make their way to job destinations. Total deaths of illegal Mexican border crossers from 2000 to February 11, 2008, have been 3,346. The greatest number of deaths takes place in Arizona because of the need to survive several days walking across the desert.[17]

What other actions would not have been necessary if illegal border crossings had been diminished? The raids on workplaces presumably would not be necessary if illegal border crossers could not easily find work in the United States. The fence along the border would be superfluous to diminish unwanted border crossings because that would have been accomplished by the lack of reward to crossing the border illegally. Separation of families would be reduced if potential illegal border crossers into the United States do not cross. The purpose of this counterfactual discussion is to give an indication of how detrimental congressional and executive ambiguity has been in not enforcing IRCA's employer-penalty provisions. The door for entry into the United States was deliberately left half open: people could cross without papers and have jobs waiting for them; and then the blame for what was taking place could be shifted to the poor Mexican whose intent was to find a better life. It has not been a story that casts glory on the United States.

Mexico-U.S. Interaction on Immigration

In February 2001, shortly after Vicente Fox assumed the presidency of Mexico, he met with President George W. Bush and the two agreed to work on immigration issues. Many senior Mexicans took this to be an opening for serious bilateral negotiations toward an immigration agreement. Jorge Castañeda, then Mexico's foreign minister, came to this conclusion; his "whole enchilada" comments came only a few months after the presidential meeting. Years later, in 2007, in an interview with the newspaper *El norte* of Monterrey, Castañeda said that negotiation on an immigration agreement was a victim of the tragic events of September 11, 2001.[18] In his 2007 book *ExMex: From Migrants to Immigrants*, Castañeda referred to the first meeting of a bilateral high-level working group on April 4, 2001, where he said there was a commitment to start migration negotiations.[19] Vicente Fox reached the same conclusion.[20] Discussion of migration is pervasive in Fox's autobiography, as it was during his six years as president of Mexico.

This belief that a migration agreement would have taken place absent President Bush's near complete dedication to the Middle East after 9/11 probably pushes too far what the pre-9/11 U.S. commitment was. There was discussion in the White House after the two presidents met and before 9/11 about how far the executive branch should stick its neck out to get a comprehensive migration agreement. Subsequent events demonstrated that high-level Mexicans and their key U.S. advisers had misread how far the U.S. Congress was prepared to go in approving a comprehensive migration agreement. In any event by pushing for everything in the migration field in the wake of the meeting between the two presidents, the Mexican government got nothing—at least at that time.

Migration relations between the two countries since then have not been felicitous. Deep divisions have prevented the U.S. Congress from enacting any new legislation. President Obama is searching to see what kinds of administrative actions he can take to improve the migration situation without legislation, at least not in his first year in office. President Calderón took the unusual step in late 2007 of criticizing U.S. presidential politics as using Mexican migrants as "thematic hostages" and deploring "the growing harassment" of Mexicans in the United States.[21] Most of the many state and local laws enacted with respect to unauthorized immigrants have been punitive.

The outstanding symbol of migration relations between the two countries is the fence under construction on the U.S. side of the border. Building the fence is detested in Mexico, and warm relations between the two countries may be impossible as long as it is there. "Walls don't work," Vicente Fox wrote in his book.[22] The fence is generally disliked by U.S. residents along the border because it is seen as interfering in the beneficial commerce that encompasses both sides and because it separates families by an artificial barrier. Mexicans also believe that it damages the environment by preventing usual movement of the region's wildlife. The fence is seen by many in the border region as a Washington imposition in an area about which Washington is uninformed and largely uncaring about the fate of the people living there.

Advocates of comprehensive immigration legislation have in mind a large, new agreement with Mexico for temporary workers. This would inevitably be pushed if the supply of unauthorized workers were drastically reduced by a combination of enhanced border security and a significant employer-penalty program. The demand of users of Mexican and Central American workers, especially in agriculture and in construction (when the U.S. housing market recovers), would be that if the unauthorized workers are not available, then they would need legal workers. In the 1970s and earlier many Mexicans came to work in U.S. agriculture during planting and harvest seasons, went home after this work was done, and then returned to the United States in the succeeding agricultural seasons. Not all those who came as ostensible temporary workers returned to Mexico, as was evident from the buildup of unauthorized workers who were legalized in the IRCA legislation. However, the coming-and-returning pattern, to the extent that it existed, became precarious after border security was enhanced in the 1990s and especially after 9/11. Getting back into the United States became too difficult, and most unauthorized workers stayed put in the United States after they came. That reality is evident by the much larger number of unauthorized workers who live in the United States today than in 1986.

There is a long history of temporary worker programs that mutate into permanent programs. Although this problem will not disappear, there undoubtedly will be much clamor for future, better organized, temporary worker programs. Some features of these programs that the U.S. government could insist on, if they are created, are reasonable wages (such as the prevailing wage rate in a region) and better working conditions than in the past. Contributions for social security coverage should be made mandatory for both employers and workers, and the buildup of contributions should be made portable. An agreement with Mexico to this effect may be required if the worker returns home in Mexico. One of the documents frequently used to demonstrate to employers that a worker is legally in the United States is a forged (or somebody else's) social security card. It is thus common that social security contributions are made for unauthorized workers who are unable to claim anything because of their status in the United States. The inability to make claims on past payments would disappear under a legalized system of temporary work.

The largest concentrations of poor people in Mexico are in rural areas. The poor include subsistence farmers but also landless peasants who seek out work as best they can. Schooling is inferior in the rural areas compared with that in large cities, and public schooling is not great even there. Consequently, there is every incentive for energetic young rural residents to leave these hopeless situations and go to Mexico's large cities or over the border into the United States. Casual observers tend to lament the visible poverty they see when they visit a place like Mexico City; they are unable to make a comparison with the more invisible poverty and lack of opportunity in isolated rural areas.

When Mexico agreed to NAFTA, the assumption was that this would enhance economic growth in urban areas. The fifteen-year phaseout of protection for significant agricultural products, such as corn, was believed to provide enough time for sufficient urban job creation to make room for immigration from rural areas. Economic growth and job creation turned out to be inadequate, however. The Mexican negotiators had it wrong, and the supporters of NAFTA in the U.S. government overestimated what Mexican job creation would be. Consequently, there were no provisions in NAFTA for resource transfers to Mexico. It is questionable that NAFTA would have been approved by the U.S. Congress had the agreement included provision for U.S. aid to Mexico—just as it is doubtful that NAFTA would have been approved if it contained provisions for substantial labor migration from Mexico to the United States. Labor usage and migration are part of the same process, but the issues are not dealt with that way by congressional committees.

There is little disposition in the U.S. Congress to provide significant aid to Mexico, although assistance is now being provided for antinarcotics cooperation. Despite this reluctance, it would be useful to analyze what techniques might work to reduce the pressure to emigrate from the Mexican countryside, via large cities, to the United States. One possibility—and surely others exist—is to provide meaningful financial assistance to set up clusters of manufacturing and service activities in regional centers in the areas from which there is considerable original emigration. This could create local jobs. This aid should be conditional on Mexico taking action on its own to support regional job-creating centers. A possible Mexican counterpart action could be to increase tax collections devoted to establishing the regional centers.[23]

Mexican dependence on the United States is more clearly demonstrated by emigration flows than by any other phenomenon. President Calderón has said accurately (and repeatedly) that the solution to stanch large-scale emigration is higher economic growth in Mexico than has been achieved during the past thirty years. Without the escape valve of emigration, internal tensions would have been much greater in Mexico. If U.S. policy drastically curtails the flow of immigrants over the next few years, this could raise internal dissatisfaction because of inadequate internal job creation. Would cutting off the flow of unauthorized entries into the United States, without an offsetting temporary worker program, stimulate the Mexican government and legislature to make the structural changes necessary to raise economic growth rates? The question is raised here, but the answer is by no means clear.

Fertility rates have declined in Mexico since the 1960s, at least outside the areas of deep poverty, and this demographic change is reducing the pressure to emigrate. Nevertheless, the early years of the twenty-first century have been the period of greatest annual Mexican immigration ever into the United States. The demographic transition surely will have greater effect over time as the number of job seekers decreases, but it is uncertain how long it will take—twenty or so more years until Mexico's demographic dividend runs its course?—to see the evidence of a demographically driven emigration decrease.

The response of repeated Mexican governments to their inability to create enough well-paying jobs to keep its young people at home is that the jobs the unauthorized immigrants do benefit the U.S. economy. That may be correct, although the evidence is by no means conclusive whether these unauthorized workers help or burden the U.S. economy. This, in any event, is for the U.S. population to decide through its political processes. Does the presence of unauthorized immigrants lower the wages of similarly skilled U.S. workers? Again, the evidence is not conclusive. Does their presence slow down the technological process of creating machines to do the work of planting and harvesting? The answer is probably "yes."[24] Do they disrupt many U.S. communities? We know from legislative proposals throughout the United States that many communities believe the answer is "yes."

The United States does not always know how to respond to the large inflow of Mexicans, especially the illegal border crossers. At times the response to Mexican workers is welcoming, as under the bracero program; and at other times it is restrictive, as the idea of the border fence shows. The U.S. response can also be extremely harsh, such as treating unauthorized immigrants as criminals; their criminal offenses are either entry into the United States without permission or using false documents to obtain jobs. This is done even when it is known that they are not criminals in the sense of harming others—they are jobseekers.

The appropriate manner in which the United States and Mexico should interact in setting migration policy that deeply affects both countries is an issue in process. In a sense it is almost always in process because it is ever-changing. The Mexican government is the supplicant in this process, and the U.S. government is the dominant player. This may change one day, when Mexico loses its worker surplus and the United States has insufficient people in its labor force to fill all the necessary jobs—but for now, the relationship in the area of migration is clearly a dependent country dealing with a dominant nation.

Migration: A Consequence of Inequality

1942
- August 4: To compensate for the shortage of agricultural workers in the United States because of World War II, the bracero program is started, which brings temporary Mexican workers to the United States.

1951
- July 12: During the Korean War the U.S. Congress passes Public Law 78 to give the bracero program permanent statutory status.

1952
- March 20: The U.S. Congress passes the McCarren-Walter immigration act, designed to deal with illegal immigration and establishing conditions on visa issuance. The act includes the so-called Texas proviso, which explicitly prohibits prosecution of employers for hiring undocumented workers.

1954
- June 17: The Immigration and Naturalization Service (INS) launches Operation Wetback, instituting stricter border controls and rounding up undocumented immigrants, while also increasing the number of braceros to between 400,000 and 450,000 annually.

1964
- December 31: The bracero program is allowed to expire in the face of criticism by U.S. labor and human rights groups about the low wages and poor working conditions of braceros.

1965
- October 3: Important amendments are passed to the Immigration and Nationality Act. Among the new provisions are capping the number of immigrants from the Western Hemisphere at 120,000 annually and making family reunification a priority for legal immigration.

1977
- Following a lawsuit by Mexican plaintiffs, the Silva program temporar-

ily (until 1981) set aside 144,946 visas for Mexicans in addition to the 120,000 hemispheric quota.

1978

- October: President Jimmy Carter establishes the Select Commission on Immigration and Refugee Policy (known as the Hesburgh Commission, after its chair, Father Hesburgh, the president of Notre Dame University) to make recommendations on immigration legislation.

1978–1980

- The Western Hemisphere cap is put at 290,000 visas, incorporating the Silva program, which is allowed to expire, and this cap is reduced to 270,000 visas in 1980. Caps are also imposed on worldwide visa issuance.

1980

- April–October: The Mariel boatlift from Cuba brings 125,000 Cubans to the United States.

1982

- June 15: The U.S. Supreme Court in *Plyler v. Doe* strikes down a Texas law allowing the state to withhold funds from local school districts that are educating undocumented migrant children. One aspect of the Court's extralegal reasoning is that these children are likely to spend their lives in the United States and should be educated to promote the national interest. The legal reason given was that these children are people and should be afforded Fourteenth Amendment protections.

1986

- November 6: The Immigration Reform and Control Act (IRCA) is passed. The grand deal in IRCA is to provide legal status to some 2.3 million undocumented immigrants who had been in the United States for at least four years and to temporary agricultural workers. IRCA provides a way to prevent a further buildup of undocumented immigrants by instituting penalties for employers who "knowingly" hire undocumented workers. The identification documents that could be used for employers to knowingly refrain from hiring undocumented immigrants are of a kind that could be readily forged (such as Social Security cards and birth certificates), however, and an industry making these forgeries quickly develops. The U.S. Congress specifically rejects instituting a foolproof identity card.

1990

- November 29: The Immigration Act of 1990 (IMMACT) is passed. The law, among other provisions, increases border security, authorizes a thousand new border patrol agents, and establishes a flexible cap of 480,000 a year for legal immigrants.

1993
- September: President Bill Clinton's administration institutes Operation Hold-the-Line, upgrading border control technology in the El Paso–Ciudad Juárez area.

1994
- January 1: NAFTA goes into effect. One of the arguments used to secure its passage in the U.S. Congress is that NAFTA would enable Mexico to "export goods and not people."
- November 8: Proposition 187 passes in California, allowing denial of social services, health care, and education to unauthorized immigrants. A federal judge issues a restraining order against the law, and it is effectively killed when Governor Pete Wilson leaves office in 1998.

1996
- April: Two incidents in Riverside County, California, receive extensive publicity and evoke considerable outrage in Mexico.
- April 1: The first is a high-speed chase, photographed by helicopter by a Los Angeles television station, after which two sheriff's deputies are seen using clubs to beat two Mexicans, a man and a woman.
- April 6: In the second incident seven Mexicans are killed when a speeding truck trying to get away from the U.S. Border Patrol crashes and turns over.
- September 30: The Illegal Immigration Reform and Immigrant Responsibility Act authorizes new funding for sophisticated technology at the border and streamlines deportation procedures for unauthorized immigrants.
- December 10: The Mexican congress approves a constitutional amendment that permits millions of Mexicans abroad to have dual nationality. Absentee voting, which is inherent in this legislation, is delayed until 2006 because of political and technical problems.

1997
- September 3: A binational study entitled *Migration between Mexico and the United States* is released by the Mexican Ministry of Foreign Affairs and the U.S. Commission on Immigration Reform. The study was suggested by Mexico and involved twenty researchers, ten from each country.

2001

- February 16: Presidents Vicente Fox and George W. Bush meet in San Cristóbal, Mexico, and release the Guanajuato Proposal under which they pledged to work on immigration and labor issues affecting both countries.
- May 21: The Development, Relief, and Education for Alien Minors Act (known as the DREAM Act) is proposed. The act would allow high-achieving high-school students who are unauthorized immigrants long-established in the United States to attend college to gain legal status. Those wishing to serve in the armed forces would also be given legal status. A successful filibuster prevented a vote on the act on October 24, 2007.
- June 21: The Mexican foreign minister Jorge Castañeda tells a group of journalists in Phoenix, Arizona, that Mexico wants "the whole enchilada or nothing" in immigration agreements between the two countries. This would consist of comprehensive U.S. immigration reform, a path to legalization for undocumented immigrants in the United States, and a temporary worker program.

2002

- May 14: Bush signs into law the Enhanced Border Security and Visa Entry Reform Act. The act authorizes increased funding for personnel at the border, requires the use of biometric identifiers on travel documents of aliens entering the United States, and seeks to coordinate information obtained by U.S. border security agencies.
- November 25: The Homeland Security Bill is signed into law. The INS functions are assigned to two bureaus of the new department: one on border security and the second on Immigration and Citizenship Enforcement (ICE).

2005

- February 10: The Agricultural Job Opportunities, Benefits, and Security Act (S. 1038, H.R. 2414, the AgJOBS Act of 2009) is proposed. The bill, as later reintroduced, would provide a two-step path to legalization, the first an "earned adjustment" of status for undocumented farm workers to be followed over the next three to five years if there is continued employment in agriculture by granting resident immigrant status (a green card). As of mid-2009, the legislation has not been passed (it has been referred to the Senate Judiciary Committee).

- April: A few hundred private individuals establish the Minutemen Project for volunteers to work alongside the U.S. Border Patrol to detect illegal border crossers.
- May 11: The REAL ID Act is attached as a rider to another bill by Congressman James Sensenbrenner (R-Wisconsin), calling for stricter documentation before a state can issue a driver's permit.
- May 12: Senators John McCain (R-Arizona) and Ted Kennedy (D-Massachusetts) propose legislation to provide a path to legalization for undocumented workers living in the United States, a guest worker program, and increased funding for border enforcement. Opponents labeled the legalization proposals as "amnesty" and prevented an actual vote in the Senate.
- July 20: Senators John Cornyn (R-Texas) and Jon Kyl (R-Arizona) propose a bill that, among other provisions, would require illegal aliens residing in the United States to leave the country and then seek legal readmission if they wish to attain legal status. This proposal never made it out of committee.
- December 6: A bill proposed by Congressman Sensenbrenner would change undocumented immigration from a civil to a criminal offense. The bill passed in the House but found insufficient support in the Senate.

2005–2008

- State and local laws and ordinances targeting unauthorized immigrants proliferate. Among other provisions, the laws seek to prohibit public benefits to these immigrants, such as issuance of a driver's license, disallowing residential renting to them, and preventing gatherings of immigrants seeking work for the day. Other efforts include enacting English-only requirements for local and state documents.

2006

- May: Bush announces Operation Jump Start, under which about six thousand National Guard troops are assigned to help the border patrol on nonenforcement tasks until more border patrol agents could be hired and trained. The National Guard troops are withdrawn from the border on July 15, 2008.
- October 26: Bush signs the Secure Fence Act for the construction of hundreds of miles of additional fencing along the U.S.-Mexico border.

2007

- March 14: President Felipe Calderón criticizes the United States for its

plans to build the seven-hundred-mile fence along the border when
he meets with Bush in Mérida, Yucatán. Calderón argues that a better
strategy would be to encourage more investment in Mexico to boost its
economy, which would slow emigration.

- May 9: Senator Majority Leader Harry Reid (D-Nevada) proposes legislation that would facilitate the legalization of unauthorized immigrants
living in the United States if they pay a two-thousand-dollar fine, pay all
taxes they owe, and travel back to their home country to apply for permanent residence (the "touchback" provision). The bill failed to attract
enough votes to invoke cloture.

2008

- July 27: The director of the Bureau of Immigration and Citizenship
Enforcement announces a program under which undocumented immigrants in the United States could come to ICE offices, be processed, and
leave the country in a few weeks without being detained. The uptake is
negligible.

2009

- April 29: During a press briefing on his hundredth day in office, President
Barack Obama says that without waiting for new immigration legislation,
he could start a more thoughtful administrative approach of giving up
raids on workplaces to detect a handful of workers. Instead, the administration would take seriously the violations of companies that sometimes
actively recruit undocumented workers.

- May 4: The U.S. Supreme Court votes unanimously to reject a tool used
against undocumented workers of charging them with "aggravated identity theft" if they used fake Social Security numbers, unless the prosecution could show that the workers knew that the numbers used belonged
to real persons. Prosecutors had threatened the charge of aggravated
identity theft, which is subject to a two-year sentence, to convince undocumented workers caught in a highly publicized raid on a meat-
packing plant in Iowa in May 2008 to plead guilty to a lesser charge and
thus a shorter stay in prison before they were deported.

The Border
A Phenomenon of Its Own

The border should be viewed as a chain that links ever more closely two peoples who are destined by geography and history to live next to each other.
— MANUEL SUÁREZ-MIER, 2007

Efforts to bolster regulatory, enforcement, and security operations at busy borders may result in a cure worse than the disease. Such endeavors place governments on a collision course with easy trade.
— STEPHEN E. FLYNN, 2000

There are close to one million legal border crossings daily between Mexico and the United States, which is more than between any other two countries.[1] About five million cargo trucks cross from Mexico each year into the zone where their cargo must be reloaded onto U.S. trucks.[2] Many people with green cards (legal residents of the United States) live in Mexico and cross the border repeatedly to work in the United States; others come to shop, for health care, and for family visits. In addition to the legal crossings from Mexico into the United States, there has been a steady flow of undocumented immigrants. One assessment is that more than half of the estimated 7.3 million Mexican immigrant entries into the United States between 2000 and 2007 were unauthorized.[3] The paraphernalia used at the border to facilitate this clandestine inflow (tunnels, safe houses, and transfer points to move the immigrants deeper into the United States) and to slow down this human inflow (border patrol, detection equipment, and detention facilities) is vast.

The Busy Border

The Mexico-U.S. border is a bottleneck.[4] One reason for this has been the large expansion of trade between Mexico and the United States under NAFTA, which increased both the population and income of Mexico's border states more than any other region of the country. The border region's gross domestic product grew by 57 percent from 1993 (the year before NAFTA went into effect) to 2004, compared with GDP growth of 30 percent for the rest of the country. From 2000 to 2005, Mexico's population grew by 1.1 percent, while that of Baja California Norte grew by 2.7 percent, Tamaulipas by almost 2 percent, and Nuevo León by 1.7 percent.[5]

A more important reason for border bottlenecks was the security measures instituted after the terror attacks of September 11, 2001. The southern and northern borders of the United States were closed for a short time after 9/11; this wreaked havoc on the just-in-time (JIT) inventory arrangements between Canada and the United States in some critical industries. For example, U.S. automotive assembly plants in Detroit had tolerances of less than an hour for receiving inputs from just across the Peace Bridge in Windsor, Ontario. If the inputs did not arrive within the specified time, assembly plants had to shut down. Similar but less-developed JIT systems for coproduction and accompanying trade in intermediate products exist between Mexico and the United States. What became evident both in Canada and the United States was that if disruptions continued, the plants producing inputs would probably have to move across the border to have the entire operation in the United States. It is not surprising, therefore, that Canada and the United States worked out a "smart border" agreement a few months later in December 2001. A comparable agreement was concluded between the United States and Mexico in early 2002.

The U.S. Department of Homeland Security (DHS) stated in one of its early reports on the Mexico-U.S. Border Partnership that it was seeking "a balance between efficiency and security" and outlined the measures taken by each country for the secure flows of people and goods.[6] The results vary among border-crossing points and the time of day that border crossing takes place. The following is a summary from one study of the time it takes for northbound passengers at major border-crossing points: Tijuana, 60 percent of pedestrians get across within one hour, but only 3 percent of passenger vehicles make it across in one hour; at Nogales, 57 percent of pedestrians and 9 percent of passenger vehicles get across within an hour; at Ciudad Juárez, the one-hour figures are 75 percent of pedestrians and 4 percent of passenger vehicles; at Nuevo Laredo, 70 percent pedestrians and 17 percent of passenger vehicles. In most cases passenger vehicles make it across within two hours.[7] The average wait times for the 3,334,026 trucks heading north in 2007 at the following four border-crossing points were: Tijuana, 745,974 trucks, 3 hours; Ciudad Juárez, 773,265 trucks, 2.2 hours; Nuevo Laredo, 1,526,623 trucks, 2.9 hours; and Nogales, 288,164 trucks, 1.1 hours.[8]

Mexican authorities believed before 9/11 that they were close to an immigration agreement with the United States and that these hopes were delayed (perhaps dashed) after that day's terrorism altered U.S. priorities. Ever since, Mexico has sought to separate the migration agenda from that on security.[9] Edward Alden, a onetime economic journalist and current senior fellow at the Council on Foreign Relations, has described how thoroughly this hope of separation failed; U.S. immigration laws were used because they permitted the authorities to legally detain and hold suspected terrorists indefinitely.[10] Alden believes that the United States has paid a high price for this procedure in that mostly innocent persons are caught. Beyond that, many highly qualified persons have elected to migrate to other locations because of the hassle they encountered at the U.S. border. The ineffectiveness of this policy may lead to what the Mexicans have long wanted—to treat antiterrorism and immigration separately.

The cliché that gained currency in the immediate aftermath of 9/11 was that "security trumps trade." This phrase was used to argue that Canada and Mexico had better "get with it" and recognize U.S. security priorities if they wished their burgeoning trade, especially after NAFTA, to continue. However, this initial macho stance gave way to the more reasonable policy of balancing trade and security. Stephen Flynn, a retired Coast Guard officer and now a leading security expert, has made major contributions to the thinking about "rebordering" North America after 9/11. Flynn made the point early on that however compelling homeland security may be, it should not be allowed to derail the continental engine of free trade. Flynn's position was that the United States should look beyond borders as a line of defense against terrorism.[11] This line of thinking has become accepted policy.

U.S. Policy Initiatives and Mexico's Response

The United States has taken many measures related to border policy, some antedating 9/11 and others stemming from the terrorist events of that day. A timeline of actions appears at the end of this chapter. Some of these actions have been useful (such as preclearance of cargo away from borders for regular shippers known to customs agents), but others are troublesome (such as the time required to move trucks and passenger cars across the U.S. border). The most important actions deal primarily with trade, narcotraffic, and migration, and they are discussed in the respective chapters dealing with these subjects. However, the border is still the most important locus for these actions because the United States and Mexico have not been able to move many necessary actions away from the border.[12]

Flynn, in an article published before 9/11, suggested that trade enforcement and security operations be moved away from busy borders well before merchandise arrived in order to speed the process.[13] American Gary Hufbauer and Mexican Gustavo Vega Cánovas wrote a widely cited article in 2003 recommending a common frontier for border management, common defense, and immigration.[14] They also recommended inspection by U.S. customs agents in foreign ports of containers that would then be sealed and made tamper-proof. A container security initiative was actually started in 2002 by U.S. Customs and Border Protection (CPB), a unit of the Department of Homeland Security, for preclearance and sealing of cargo containers in foreign ports. CPB reports that fifty-eight such arrangements are operational.[15]

An independent task force of the Council on Foreign Relations made an even more ambitious recommendation for unclogging bottlenecks at the two internal borders in North America (those of the United States with Canada and Mexico)—namely, to establish a common security perimeter by 2010.[16] The report was published in 2005, and there has been no progress thus far in the direction proposed. If there is to be free flow of people within a common security perimeter, as the report recommends, this implies common immigration policies because entry into any of the countries would give access to all three. If goods are to be cleared at the perimeter and are then free to flow into any of the three countries, as was recommended in the report, this requires a common external tariff—as would be the case if NAFTA were transformed from a free-trade area into a customs union. A common security perimeter is unlikely in the immediate future.

The Security and Prosperity Partnership (SPP) agreement that preceded the report from the Council on Foreign Relations—indeed, the latter report stated that it was building on the SPP—is much less ambitious. The SPP was not intended to lead to three-country legislation or executive agreements, but rather to function within existing legal and administrative authorities. Indeed,

Congress was excluded from the SPP process in the United States. Instead, the SPP was set up to work through twenty working groups and annual summit meetings of the leaders of Canada, Mexico, and the United States. However, its accomplishments before its abolition in 2009 were modest.[17]

The idea of virtual clearance of cargo away from the border has now become part of the balance to accomplish both security and trade objectives. The most far-reaching proposals, such as those for setting up perimeter security encompassing the three countries, have not prospered—or perhaps, not yet. The two smart-border agreements concluded in the immediate aftermath of 9/11 were bilateral. The Canada-U.S. agreement came first, and this has been the traditional path—Canada first—for policy innovations in North America.[18] The preclearance measures now in place undoubtedly have reduced the time that would otherwise have been taken post-9/11 for containers and trucks to clear U.S. customs, agricultural, and security inspections. However, these measures are by no means optimal. The security aspect of border control adds expense to the movement of cargo. U.S. unwillingness to allow Mexican cargo trucks to travel to the ultimate destination in the United States, despite the commitment made in NAFTA to do precisely this, adds to the expense of transporting goods. The Mexicans retaliated by imposing similar restrictions on U.S. trucks bringing cargo into Mexico.

The infrastructure at the border, especially on the Mexican side, is deficient, adding to the time and cost to move goods.[19] The U.S. Department of Transportation (DOT) has estimated that practices of Mexican customs brokers, particularly for cargo moving into the interior of Mexico, results in holding the cargo in a Mexican warehouse from three to five days before it is released to continue the southward journey.[20] Canada, Mexico, and the United States have different weight and size regulations for trucks, and each country has a different methodology to calculate maximum limits. The existence of boundaries therefore represents a large obstacle for truck movement. The transport and logistics expert Juan Carlos Villa has commented that perhaps the simplest way to harmonize truck regulations is for the other two countries to adopt U.S. standards, because the United States has the largest industry, but both Mexico and Canada have higher gross vehicle weight allowances than the United States.[21] The North American Steel Trade Committee (NASTC), which worked under the aegis of the SPP, has argued that intra-NAFTA steel shippers must conform to the lightest weight allowance of the three countries and therefore must send a larger number of single truck loads than would be the case if they could use trucks with higher weight allowances. This leads to higher shipment costs for steel and other commodities.[22]

The primary purposes of NAFTA in terms of Mexico-U.S. interaction were to augment trade between the two countries and to encourage foreign direct investment (FDI) flows into Mexico.[23] Both these objectives were accomplished. The initial stimulus for increasing intra–North American trade was the combination of the gradual elimination of tariffs and other border barriers and the fact that most other countries had to pay normal tariffs on the goods they exported to North American countries (that is, the most-favored-nation tariff). The preferential aspect of this arrangement diminished over the years because both Mexico and the United States concluded free trade agreements (FTAs) with many other countries. North American free trade continued, but it lost its exclusivity. This affected many industries. In the early years after NAFTA went into effect, Mexico became an important exporter of clothing to the United States. As the preferential advantage diminished, Mexico's clothing exports declined.[24]

Beyond losing its preferential exclusivity, the security measures put in place at the U.S. border reduced the competitive benefit of proximity that Mexico enjoys. So close to the United States, but so far away procedurally. As trucks took longer to cross the border, this disrupted the competitive benefits of just-in-time inventory systems. Longer waiting times increased costs. So did the inability of Mexican trucks to deliver goods to the destination in the United States, an impediment that Canadian trucks do not face. Instead of one driver, shipment of Mexican goods by truck requires three drivers. When these extra costs are added, the use of the words "free trade" is fiction. It is not surprising that the proportion of goods shipped to the United States from Mexico by truck diminished from 73 percent of the total in 1999 to an estimated 66 percent in 2006.[25]

The Trucking Dispute

The trucking dispute between Mexico and the United States is primarily a story of the power of U.S. lobbyists in overturning a formal commitment entered into by the two governments in NAFTA. This was accompanied by lobbying by Mexican companies that benefited from the U.S. violation of its commitments and apparently reduced the vigor of the Mexican government in its protests against the U.S. action. There were two NAFTA provisions regarding the right of Mexican trucks to carry cargo into the United States. The first specified that within three years after NAFTA was signed on December 17, 1992, Mexican trucks would be allowed access to the four U.S. border states—Arizona, California, New Mexico, and Texas. It had always been understood that Mexican trucks and drivers would have to comply with state and U.S. safety standards.

On December 18, 1995, however, the U.S. Department of Transportation announced a delay in the implementation of this provision. The delay followed heavy lobbying by the Teamsters Union. The Teamsters had filed suit three days earlier alleging inadequate safety standards of Mexican trucks and drivers. The delay in giving Mexican trucks full access to the four U.S. border states meant that trucks could carry cargo only into a "commercial zone" extending about twenty miles on either side of the border, where the cargo had to be transferred to a U.S. truck. In July 1998, almost three years later, Mexico requested a meeting of the Free Trade Commission of NAFTA, made up of the ministers responsible for trade of the three countries. The commission was unable to resolve the dispute.

The second provision in NAFTA was that six years after the agreement went into effect (which was on January 1, 1994), Mexican trucks would be allowed to carry cargo to destinations throughout the United States. When the time for this came, on January 1, 2000, the United States again refused to honor the agreement. In February 2001 a NAFTA dispute-settlement panel found that the U.S. refusal to review and consider for approval Mexican truck license applications was in breach of U.S. obligations under Annex 1 of the agreement. This ruling gave Mexico the right to retaliate against U.S. imports, but this right was not exercised—at least not until March 19, 2009. President George W. Bush pledged to open discussions with Mexico to implement the panel decision. The U.S. Congress responded by mandating twenty-two additional safety measures, and in November 2002 the Department of Transportation certified that many Mexican truckers had complied with all of these. Bush lifted the moratorium and instructed the Federal Motor Carrier Safety Administration (FMCSA) to start processing applications from Mexican trucking firms that had received licenses.

In January 2003 another roadblock emerged when the Teamsters, the interest group Public Citizen (which had opposed NAFTA from the outset), and other labor and environmental organizations challenged the decision to permit Mexican trucks to travel throughout the United States. This challenge called for a delay in implementation of the decision because the U.S. government had not complied with environmental impact statement requirements under the National Environmental Protection Act (NEPA). The Ninth Circuit Court of Appeals, in *Public Citizen v. Department of Transportation* on February 16, 2003, delayed the implementation of U.S. trucking obligations pending completion of environmental impact reviews. In June 2004 the U.S. Supreme Court unanimously overturned this decision and found that the FMCSA did not violate NEPA.

In February 2007 the DOT announced a one-year pilot program to give one hundred Mexican companies unrestricted access to U.S. roadways, with reciprocal access to be given to Mexican roadways by one hundred U.S. companies. In May 2007 a provision was added to an unrelated appropriations bill to block funds until the DOT published details on the program and allowed time for public comment. It took until September 6, 2007, before the DOT was able to put the pilot program in place. In July 2008 the DOT announced that it would extend the pilot program for another two years. Twenty-seven Mexican trucking companies (101 trucks) and ten U.S. companies (52 trucks) had been granted access under the program as of mid-September 2008, and forty additional Mexican carriers had passed a preauthorization safety audit. Efforts continued to be made in the U.S. Congress to cut off funds for the pilot program, but without success until March 2009, when the funds were eliminated from the U.S. government's budget.

No credible evidence has been presented that Mexican drivers pose a greater safety risk than U.S. drivers. Indeed, the evidence is just the opposite. This evidence comes from FMCSA's safety database.[26] The U.S. government had two years to deal with the driver safety issue about access to U.S. border states, but the decision not to honor the agreement in NAFTA came only on the eve of implementation. The later decision on access by Mexican trucks to the entire country still has not been dealt with eight-and-a-half years after the agreed date other than by the now canceled temporary program. Many Mexicans see little hope that the U.S. Congress will ever agree to implement the U.S. NAFTA commitment; they expected a partial solution to be a gradual extension of the temporary program to more Mexican trucks and drivers over many more years. This outcome was dashed, however, when the U.S. government terminated the funding for the temporary program.

The way the system now works is that a Mexican truck brings the goods to the border, where it is inspected by Mexican authorities and then brought into the border commercial zone. At that point the trailer is picked up by a drayage truck, a short-haul vehicle, and brought to the U.S. side of the border to a drop lot, where the trailer is picked up by a U.S. long-haul driver to be brought to its destination. Each shipment thus involves three trucks and three drivers. Long-haul trucks are generally not used by Mexican trucking companies to bring the cargo to the border because the hauls are not generally long. The Mexican trucks used in the temporary program, by contrast, had to meet U.S. standards. The argument used by Public Citizen in its lawsuit that was decided by the Supreme Court in 2004 implicitly says that the use of Mexican trucks and drivers to bring goods to the destination in the United States could result in environmental damage. The logic seems to be just the reverse—using three trucks, including drayage trucks that are unlikely to be environmentally friendly given the nature of the task assigned to them, and involving long waits at the border—namely, that bringing the cargo in modern, preinspected Mexican trucks to the destination of the cargo would be more environmentally sound.

A 2005 report by Juan Carlos Villa provides a detailed listing of the issues involved in truck movement of cargo. Some favorable points exist, such as a single inspection by the three agencies involved (for security, customs, and agriculture), advance transmission electronically of cargo information, clarifying inspection regulations, and the informal coordination of inspectors on both sides of the border. Villa also lists defects in the process beyond those discussed earlier, such as disparate U.S. and Mexican laws on trucks, disparities between shipping schedules and operating hours at ports of entry, lack of communication to drivers about port-of-entry operations, and concentration of traffic at few ports of entry.[27]

The fee for the decoupling of trailers in the designated commercial zone and the movement of the trailers by drayage trucks apparently varies between $100 and $150. The number of trucks crossing from Mexico to the United States in 2006 was 4.76 million; however, about 10 percent to 20 percent were "bobtails"—that is, tractors without trailers.[28] Being conservative and using the $100 fee, and reducing the number of trailers that have to be decoupled and moved by drayage trucks by 20 percent, still comes to $381 million. This amount was the *minimum* earnings that accrued to the Mexican drayage companies in 2006. The profit explains why the drayage companies opposed the demonstration program. The beneficiaries of the current system in both countries have been able to prevent maximum efficiency in truck transportation of cargo between Mexico and the United States.[29]

For years there was much internal discussion in Mexico as to whether its government should avail itself of the authority it was given by the NAFTA trade-dispute panel to retaliate by restricting some two-billion-plus dollars of imports from the United States. Mexico chose not to do this, hoping that U.S. policy would one day be brought into line with the commitments the United States entered into in NAFTA. Mexico feared that trade retaliation would set off a major confrontation between a dependent and a more powerful country, and Mexican authorities were quite sure that they did not want this fight. Imposing import restrictions would harm the U.S. companies that export the products chosen but could also damage the importers of these products.

The United States, however, made it abundantly clear when funding for the pilot program was terminated that it had no intention of *ever* allowing Mexican trucks to bring cargo to destinations in the United States. The Mexican authorities evidently had considered what they would do if the pilot program were terminated because the list of items for trade retaliation was announced just a few days after the United States acted. The retaliation list did not include staple products the United States ships to Mexico, such as corn, but instead a variety of foodstuffs, juices, and other products that could readily be imported from other countries with which Mexico had free trade agreements so as to minimize damage to its importers. The list of products included exports from some forty U.S. states. And, as Mexico hoped, the careful choices it made led some 140 U.S. associations and businesses to sign a letter to President Obama asking that the United States live up to its obligations.

When the United States did not allow Mexican trucks to deliver cargo to destinations throughout the four U.S. border states, Mexico took similar action against U.S. trucks. Mexico refrained for more than eight years from the time that it obtained the right to retaliate against the imports of U.S. goods before it acted. If the shoe had been on the other foot, if Mexico had taken the original restrictive action against U.S. trucks or some other important service rendered by U.S. companies, the U.S. government almost certainly would have retaliated as quickly as it could. It is hard to fault the Mexican action. Mexico clearly was the aggrieved party. The U.S. government, by contrast, gave greater weight to the anticompetitive lobbying of the Teamsters Union than to obligations it had freely entered into.[30] President Obama has since said that the United States will work with Mexico to resolve the trucking/trade retaliation problem. It is not clear as this is written whether the United States hopes to restore the pilot program, live up to its commitment in NAFTA, or find another way to resolve the problem. For its part Mexican authorities have said they hope the United States will honor its NAFTA commitments so that they can remove their retaliatory trade measures.

The Border Fence

Another problem introduced by the United States is the plan to build a fence along some 700 miles of the 1,950 miles of the U.S.-Mexico border as an anti-immigration, antidrug device. The fence building has also become an antiterrorist measure.[31] If the U.S. argument is based on the fence having so many objectives, it is probably because there is nothing solid to any single purported motive. There have been problems. Property owners along the proposed route have contested the expropriation of their property without adequate compensation. Some properties would have to be split in two. There is concern at some points that the fence would impede wildlife movements from one side of the border to the other. Many mayors and governors along the border oppose the fence as detrimental to the prospering commerce on both sides. Many residents along the border who have families they visit regularly on the other side are against building the fence.[32] "Fence" or "wall"? The words are used interchangeably. Within twenty-four hours after being named the president-elect of Mexico, Felipe Calderón attacked the construction of the wall.[33]

There are other ways to deter undocumented immigration, such as actually imposing stiff penalties on employers who knowingly hire them (as discussed in chapter 6). A fence is hardly the optimal way to cut off narcotics shipments from Mexico to the United States, and it does nothing to prevent the large profits drug dealers are able to send to Mexico spawning the violence there (as discussed in chapter 4). There is no solid evidence that terrorists are entering the United States from Mexico posing as unauthorized immigrants. A 2008 article in the *Economist* has argued that as long as there is a large wage gap, Mexicans will continue to "find themselves" in the U.S. labor force.[34] The existence of a wall (or fence) between the two countries is an indication that the United States does not anticipate close relations with Mexico over time. Rather, the fence signals that the United States wants separation even as it talks about integration. Stephen Flynn has noted that great powers have been building walls throughout history—China's Great Wall, the Maginot Line, the Berlin Wall—and all have met the same dismal fate. He anticipates the same for the U.S. wall against Mexico.[35]

The behavior of the two countries at their common border is consistent with the key hypothesis of the research—namely, that Mexico for many years acted as the dependent country and the United States as the dominant one. NAFTA was groundbreaking in that it was the first comprehensive trade agreement that brought together an advanced, high-wage country and an economically weaker, low-wage nation. The European Union at that time included countries with large income and wage disparities, but not as great as between the United States and Mexico. That originality was also NAFTA's weakness in that it brought out fears of many U.S. workers, producers, and communities about the low-wage competition they would face.

The case in favor of free trade was made by the economically weaker and dependent country. Under the dependency-dominance hypothesis, one would have expected the stronger country to propose free trade. President Carlos Salinas's original proposal was not for free trade across-the-board, but rather for free trade in specific sectors. This broke down quickly because each country wanted to negotiate in those sectors in which it believed it had or would develop a competitive advantage. Canada, before it entered into its free trade agreement with the United States, also proposed sector agreements. Both countries, Mexico and Canada before it, realized that comprehensive negotiations permitted de facto but unspecified trade-offs among many or all sectors. The trucking provisions of NAFTA made it into the agreement on that basis; a trucking agreement opening the two countries completely to the trucks of the other almost certainly could not have been successfully completed except in the wider context of economic integration.

The trucking agreement broke down when the time came for implementation. The breakdown took place on the U.S. side. The idea of a trial trucking program was also anathema by the U.S. opponents of NAFTA, and they were supported by their congressional allies. It is remarkable that the trial program was able to proceed as long as it did in the face of congressional efforts to cut the funding for it. The protectionist behavior of the dominant power took place in the U.S. Congress, not at first in the U.S government; but in the end the U.S. president, without comment, signed the bill containing the protectionist congressional action. The Mexicans behaved as one would have expected in the face of the U.S. unwillingness to live up to its commitments—the Mexicans delayed responding at each step. But in this area, as in many others, the Mexicans became more assertive when it was evident that further patience was not a winning strategy.

The United States, the government and the legislature, acted as the dominant players when decisions were made to erect a fence along the Mexican border and to lengthen its coverage. However, Mexico had changed. The new president-elect, Felipe Calderón, spoke out against the fence in one of his first official statements after he took office in 2006. Mexico is becoming more assertive in criticizing U.S. border actions in much the same way it has regarding U.S. antinarcotics policy. U.S.-Mexico actions at the border differ from the other five policy chapters (trade, foreign direct investment and finance, narcotics, energy, and migration) in that they deal with a region where the two countries come together rather than with specific sectors or programs. The border was included in the analysis in this book precisely because its nature is different from the other five areas, but also because the patterns of policymaking by the two countries with respect to the border are much the same as in their interactions in specific sectors.

The Border: A Phenomenon of Its Own

1983

- August 14: Presidents Ronald Reagan of the United States and Miguel de la Madrid of Mexico sign the La Paz Agreement, addressing pollution and environmental problems along the Mexico-U.S. border. The border is defined as 100 kilometers on either side.

1991

- January: U.S. Navy Seabees build a ten-foot-high wall extending seven miles along the Chula Vista–Tijuana border.

1992

- February: The Integrated Border Development Plan is released by the U.S. Environmental Protection Agency and the Mexican secretariat of urban development and ecology.

1993

- October: The steel wall built by the Seabees in 1991 is extended to fourteen miles in length, to the Pacific Ocean.
- September: Operation Hold-the-Line (originally named Operation Blockade) is enforced by the Immigration and Naturalization Service to curb the flow of undocumented immigrants in the El Paso, Texas, area.
- November: The Mexican and U.S. governments create the Border Environmental Cooperation Commission (BECC) and the North American

Development Bank (NADBank) as add-ons to NAFTA. BECC's role is to certify environmental aspects of projects and that of the NADBank to finance them.

- Operation Gatekeeper, increasing technology and the police presence, is instituted in California. The program is designed to divert undocumented migrants from crossing the border into the San Diego area.
- Operation Safeguard is instituted to increase security along three hundred miles of the Arizona-Mexico border.

1995
- December 18: The U.S. Secretary of Transportation announced a delay in allowing Mexican trucks to cross into the four U.S. border states despite the agreement that this would be permitted three years after NAFTA was signed on December 17, 1992. The ostensible reason for the executive order was the lack of safety of Mexican trucks and drivers. Much pressure for the U.S. action came from the Teamsters Union. Mexico responded by delaying access to U.S. trucks coming into its territory.

2000
- January 1: Under NAFTA, Mexican trucks were supposed to have full access to the United States six years after the agreement went into effect on January 1, 1994. The United States did not honor this agreement on the same grounds that the earlier provision had been delayed in 1995. Access by Mexican trucks carrying cargo to destinations in the United States is still disallowed as this is written in mid-2009.

2002
- March: The U.S.-Mexico Smart Border Accord is signed.

2003
- January 24: The U.S. Department of Homeland Security (DHS) begins to operate.
- April: DHS launches US VISIT to verify identification of individuals coming to the United States for work, study, or travel.
- September 2: DHS announces a new initiative known as "One Face at the Border" to unify the inspection process at the border rather than continue the separate screenings by immigration, customs, and agricultural inspectors.
- September 27: The Free and Secure Trade (FAST) initiative between Mexico and the United States comes into effect beginning with the Ciudad Juárez, Chihuahua–El Paso, Texas, port. The initiative is intended to

speed processing of cargo by allowing importers and carriers enrolled in the Customs Trade Partnership Against Terrorism (C-PAT) to use fast lanes with less extensive physical examination of contents.

2004

- October 8: Mexico's secretariat of foreign relations publishes a note condemning violations of human rights occurring at the U.S. border, noting in particular the more than three thousand migrant deaths that have resulted from the United States's Operation Guardian.

2005

- January 31: The Law of National Security (the Ley de Seguridad Nacional) is published in the *Diario official*, which establishes a Mexican National Security Council.
- March 23: Mexico, Canada, and the United States announce the formation of the Security and Prosperity Partnership of North America (SPP).

2006

- President Bush announces Operation Jump Start to deploy six thousand National Guard troops to work with the U.S. Border Patrol.
- October 26: Bush signs the Secure Fence Act, calling for seven hundred miles of fencing along the border.

2007

- September 6: The U.S. Department of Transportation puts into effect a pilot program for Mexican companies that are cleared to carry cargo directly to purchasers in the United States. This was done despite the opposition of many members of the U.S. Congress. The companies operating from Mexico must pass a preauthorization safety audit before they are granted access to the United States.

2009

- March 11: President Barack Obama signs the Omnibus Appropriations Bill, which includes a provision to terminate funding for the pilot program for trucks put into effect by the United States in September 2007.
- March 19: Mexico puts into effect import tariff increases of 10 percent to 45 percent for eighty-nine products exported by the United States.
- April 7: More than 140 business associations, producers, and exporters send a letter to Obama urging him to work with the U.S. Congress and with Mexico to resolve the trucking dispute that led Mexico to increase its import restrictions on U.S. products.

Findings
Changing Traditional Practices

A
s one examines the elements that went into the bilateral policymaking regarding the issues discussed throughout this book, it is clear that Mexico has historically behaved in a dependent fashion with the United States as the dominant nation. Dependence has produced defensive behavior on the part of Mexico. On trade policy Mexico adopted import-substituting industrialization (ISI) in large part to minimize the influence of the "hegemon to the north" (Carlos Salinas's words), and long shunned direct negotiation with the United States. On foreign direct investment (FDI) the pattern was to limit and regulate the extent of foreign (mostly U.S.) equity participation in favor of debt financing to obtain the necessary capital inflows to develop Mexico's manufacturing and service activities. On banking the pattern was to limit the role of foreign-owned banks and insurance companies. On narcotics Mexico's policy on interdiction, spraying crops, and living with the annual certification procedure was largely determined by U.S. policy.[1]

On energy Mexico to this day allows no private equity investment for oil exploration, production, and marketing. Mexico has refrained from having a public position on U.S. immigration laws and regulations, ostensibly based on the rationale of not interfering in the internal affairs of another nation. Finally, while displeased with U.S. behavior at the border of conflating immigration and security policy and refusing to allow Mexican long-haul trucks to carry cargo to U.S. destinations, Mexico was not assertive in countering these decisions for more than a decade.

U.S. policies toward Mexico on these issues were generally aggressive, as befits a dominant power. There was little the U.S. government could do to change Mexico's inward-looking trade policy, but there was perennial preaching about the benefits to Mexico to open its market. The United States followed the same approach on FDI, and the lecturing about the benefits of attracting FDI was accompanied by private companies seeking to invest in Mexico. On narcotics U.S. policy pushed as much of the blame for the high U.S. consumption on Mexico's failure to interdict drugs before they entered the United States—even as the United States was no more successful in drug interdiction in its territory. There was a steady flow of official and private U.S. statements about the advantages for Mexico to allow private equity investment in the exploration for oil.

The United States de facto has long welcomed immigrants to come to work in agriculture, construction, and many service activities, with or without prior authorization, and then shifted policy to punish "illegal" Mexican immigrants when too many came. Most Mexicans hate the fence going up on the U.S. side of the border, but they were not meaningfully asked for their opinions. In fact, neither were most U.S. officials in border cities and states asked to provide their judgments about the fence. The U.S. government broke its agreement in NAFTA to allow Mexican long-haul trucks to bring cargo directly to the destinations in the United States.

The dependent-dominant relationship has grown out of the different histories of the two countries and dissimilar economic achievements. Dependency-dominance is not identical with asymmetry. There was asymmetry in economic and political power between the United States and just about all other countries in the world during most of the twentieth century, but give-and-take in many of these bilateral relationships was more balanced than it was between Mexico and the United States. Dependency-dominance grew out of the combination of asymmetry and proximity. Neither is dependency-dominance the consequence of a love-hate relationship—the words "love" and "hate" are proxies for other feelings, but they are too strong. However, there has been considerable American disparagement of Mexican practices, such as the country's long failure to achieve democracy, its rampant corruption, the country's high level of income inequality and of poverty, and its inability to keep a large portion of its citizenry at home. Mexicans who migrated across the border did not necessarily love the United States, but they welcomed the opportunity to improve their economic lot and that of their families.

This book emphasizes dependency-dominance because that relationship has dominated official policy for so long and permeated into the thinking of the two populations. The central objective of this analysis, as stated at the outset, is to help change the bilateral relationship into one that has a more balanced interchange. Greater actual equality will require some convergence in per capita incomes. More cooperative interchange may contribute to greater equality over time, and at its heart the purpose of the discussion is to make the day-to-day relationships more productive. The historical dependency-dominance relationships summarized in each chapter are still prevalent but have been changing. Changes have occurred at moments of stress in one or both countries. This is perhaps the book's most important conclusion as it relates to Mexico.

Changing Economic Policy

Mexico has demonstrated an ability to make a 180-degree change in economic policy in the face of a crisis. Examples of this ability are readily available. While many Mexican economists urged modification of import-substituting industrialization (ISI) policy in the late sixties and early seventies, the change did not take place until after the economic crisis of 1982. The change was profound in that it altered development policy from looking inward to focusing on export promotion, from limiting FDI to seeking it, and even unilaterally lowering import protection. In late 1994, when Mexico found that it could not refinance its *tesobonos* and the value of the peso plunged, Mexico shifted from an essentially fixed to a floating exchange rate. The limits on foreign ownership of banks during the reprivatization exercise of 1991–1992 and again in the finance provisions of NAFTA were altered during the severe financial crisis of 1994–1995, so much so that all large commercial banks now operating in Mexico, save one, are foreign-owned. When it became clear how much Mexico could be affected by the then pending U.S. Immigration Reform and

Control Act of 1986, there was a change from a "no policy" policy to active lobbying to influence that law and future U.S. immigration legislation.

Acting Assertively

Mexico's current president has demonstrated his willingness to act assertively when U.S. policy compromises Mexican national interests. The best example of this was President Felipe Calderón's request to President George W. Bush when the two met in Mérida, Yucatán, in October 2007, for a greater U.S. contribution in the joint battle against narcotrafficking and the violence it is generating in Mexico. The United States responded positively—although the promised expenditures under the Mérida Initiative have been lagging. Calderón, when he was still president-elect in 2006, criticized the U.S. plan to build a fence separating the two countries. On this, however, there was no direct U.S. response.

Resisting U.S. Pressure

Mexico has shown willingness during the past decade to resist U.S. pressure to take actions that it believes are not in Mexico's interest. The most important example of this was the refusal of President Vicente Fox to support the U.S. invasion of Iraq. Mexico and Chile, both U.S. allies, were members of the UN Security Council when the United States withdrew a resolution when it became clear that a vote in favor of the invasion would fail.[2] Another example is the continuing refusal of the Mexican congress to allow Pemex to enter into risk contracts with private and foreign companies for the exploration and production of oil, despite pressure to move in this direction. This policy has existed for seventy years.

Avoiding Failed Economic Policies

After obvious failures of existing policy, economic policy changes in Mexico have frequently led to precisely the policies that had long been resisted. This is akin to what Winston Churchill once said about the United States—that it will come to the right conclusion after all else fails. ISI was abandoned only after it led to a crisis; limiting foreign ownership of banks led after 1994 to overwhelming foreign bank ownership; resistance to an effective floating exchange rate gave way only after there was no viable option to this action; lobbying the United States on its immigration policy became the single most important issue under President Vicente Fox; and then, when this emphasis led to nothing, the current president, Felipe Calderón, played down this issue in his policy priorities.

Overcoming Special Interests

The great power of special interests in Mexico can be overcome only during a crisis. Producers of manufactured goods resisted import liberalization because ISI shielded them from foreign price and quality competition. Special tax and subsidy provisions are written into federal budgets because of the power of the influential companies that receive these benefits. President Fox made no meaningful effort to implement antimonopoly measures during his sexenio. Powerful labor unions have been able to prevent changes in labor laws that protect the benefits of their members even as they resulted in substantial informal employment for other Mexicans in the labor force. Many more examples could be cited on the durability of special interests. Mexico is not unique in this respect. Required changes in the U.S. financial sector are being addressed only now after the deep financial crisis in the country. In Mexico the power of special interests working through the political structure is the major factor preventing structural changes necessary to foster higher GDP growth and adequate job-creation.

Although Mexico is fast running out of oil, the sense of crisis is not yet acute, and Mexico's energy sector is replete with opposition to change. The labor union in Pemex long had five seats on the company's eleven-member board of directors and was able to retain these in the recent Pemex legislation because of the union's influence on Mexico's two large traditional political parties, the PAN and the PRI. Pemex has more employees relative to production than any other major oil producer. Pemex lacks the expertise for deepwater oil and gas exploration in the Gulf of Mexico, where great promise exists.

Public opinion in Mexico remains opposed to private and foreign involvement in the form of joint ventures to compensate for Pemex's lack of expertise where it is most necessary despite falling oil and gas output and declining proven reserves. Unless Mexico is extraordinarily lucky and makes an accidental find, such as that of Cantarell in the shallow waters of the Gulf of Mexico, the relevant question is, Will Mexico make the necessary changes in oil policy in anticipation of a pending oil shortage, or will it take a crisis to bring about change? If history is a guide, change will not come until the crisis; but then, if faced with the reality of an oil shortage, the probability is high that there will be an about-face in oil policy. Next are conclusions with respect to U.S. policymaking toward Mexico.

Blaming Mexico for Policy Failure

The United States is prone to blame Mexico for policy failure of its own making. Perhaps the best example of this behavior can be seen in the antidrug program as it has evolved over many years. U.S. policy failed to curb domestic demand for illicit drugs. The U.S. government response to this failure was Operation Intercept instituted in 1969 based on the conviction that slowing down vehicular traffic at the border and compromising Mexican exports would concentrate the minds of Mexican officials on the kind of antidrug efforts the United States sought from its neighbor. A second Operation Intercept took place in 1985 after DEA agent Enrique Camarena was tortured and murdered in Mexico. U.S. legislation in 1986 required the president to certify that Mexico and other Latin American countries were cooperating fully in interdicting drug shipments before they reached the U.S. border. Mexico has never been decertified, but the threat of withdrawal of U.S. economic benefits has never been absent either.

Even today, building a fence along the border with Mexico is based in part on reducing the quantity of narcotics entering into the United States. The consumption of drugs produced in and shipped through Mexico to the United States is spawning horrible violence in Mexico. The United States did little to help Mexico control this violence until Mexican president Felipe Calderón requested assistance. Even then, the U.S. Congress sought to impose conditions on granting help that is modest compared with what Mexico must spend on its own account. Little has been done to control the traffic in weapons sales from U.S. gun dealers to Mexican drug lords.

U.S. immigration legislation over many years, including IRCA in 1986, deliberately left the door half open to unauthorized Mexican immigrants; current U.S. policy is to punish the Mexicans who came through this half-open door. The failure of the Congress to honor the U.S. trucking agreement in NAFTA was blamed, without valid evidence, on faulty safety standards of Mexican long-haul trucks and drivers. A large majority of the U.S. Congress succeeded in 2009 to cut the funding for the pilot trucking program instituted by the U.S. Department of Transportation as a way to reward the Teamsters Union for its support of the Democratic Party in the 2008 elections, and without much consideration of how the Mexican government might feel about this.

Special Interests Diminishing National Welfare

Special interests diminish U.S. national welfare in much the same way as they do in Mexico. The main difference between the two countries is that the United States is richer and the population can generally more easily afford the cost of deferring to special interests than can the Mexican population—although this assertion must be tempered in the current U.S. context of a housing collapse, financial turmoil, and a weak overall economy. The United States is fostering an inefficient truck transportation system in order to prevent competition with Mexico truckers. In its search for "energy independence," the United States is subsidizing noncompetitive domestic ethanol production rather than opening its market to ethanol that can be produced more efficiently by large sugar producers in the hemisphere and elsewhere.

Efficiency: A Secondary Consideration

Efficiency is often a secondary consideration in U.S. policymaking toward Mexico. Two examples supporting this conclusion are the U.S. dismissal of the trucking agreements in NAFTA, thus forcing the use of at least three vehicles and three drivers for truck delivery of goods from Mexico to destinations in the United States, and building the fence that will slow cross-border commerce to the detriment of border cities in both countries. The burdens of U.S. security precautions at the border have diminished since 9/11 due to the Smart Border agreement and the use of special lanes for the movement of precleared cargo trucks and passenger vehicles, but the costs still largely nullify the transportation advantage Mexico has because of its proximity to the U.S. market. Just-in-time inventory arrangements exist between Mexican and U.S. producers, but they are less productive than those between Canada and the United States, where trucks can make deliveries at cross-border locations and do not have to overcome the extra security precautions that motivated the building of a fence at the Mexican border.[3]

Overcoming Impediments to Economic Development

The United States has not provided the large amounts of financial assistance needed to help Mexico overcome its impediments to economic development. NAFTA, from the outset, was seen in the United States as a stimulus to economic development resulting from trade expansion of each member country and as a way to encourage FDI into Mexico. NAFTA's organizational structure was minimal, deliberately so; and other than what was in the agreement and the side agreements on labor and the environment, there were no Mexican commitments to structural changes. Both omissions turned out to be detrimental: the first from the absence of high-level intergovernmental give-and-take on important trade issues, and the second because the political restraints in Mexico prevented the resolution of significant structural issues.[4]

The United States did agree to provide financial support to the North American Development Bank (NADBank), but the amounts appropriated by the U.S. Congress were frequently whittled down. The two countries contributed an equal amount to the original capital of NADBank, and the border environmental projects that the bank financed were split fifty-fifty between Mexico and the United States. The United States never contemplated providing financial support to undeveloped regions in Mexico as part of NAFTA. This model differed sharply from that of the European Union. U.S. financial support under the Mérida Initiative was an exception to this generalization; in this case there was an implicit threat that Mexico would reduce its antidrug cooperation if the United States did not help Mexico reduce the violence engendered by U.S. drug consumption.

If the United States was prepared to provide aid to its much poorer neighbor to foster its economic growth, many possibilities exist. Mexican infrastructure—roads, environmental projects, port facilities, and the like—are woefully inadequate. The three countries could make a weighted contribution to an infrastructure fund for use by all of them.[5] The United States could help Mexico set up clusters of manufacturing or service activities regionally to provide jobs in rural areas as an alternative to emigrating to large cities in Mexico or to the United States. Mexico should be asked to contribute to these centers with its own funds. There are many permutations of programs like these, and the necessary step before negotiation with Mexico on them is to obtain consent from the U.S. government and Congress that they are prepared to consider financial assistance—and how much. The key argument in favor of such assistance is that the greater the level of its economic growth, the more Mexico will import commercially from the United States.

Changing U.S. Policies That Conflict with Mexico's Priorities

Once they are established, it is hard to change U.S. policies that conflict with Mexico's priorities. Some examples of this are the fence along the border that is despised by Mexican authorities, the refusal to allow Mexican trucks to bring cargo to U.S. destinations (except for a few years under the limited special program), and the inability to bring more clarity to immigration policy, especially for dealing with unauthorized immigrants in the country. There is no clear indication that the United States is prepared to change key elements of the "war on drugs," such as replacing the promiscuous arrest of drug offenders by more education and treatment. Failing a change that takes away the substantial rents received from sales in the United States by drug cartels, there is little prospect that Mexico will be able to reduce its drug-related violence.

The tendency toward rigidity in existing U.S. policies toward Mexico is part of a deeper attitude of the relatively low priority the United States has placed on its relations with Mexico. If Mexico had a more prominent place in U.S. foreign policy, more official attention would be given to changing actions that are anathema to Mexico, such as those cited here. It may not be clear to most U.S. officials or to the men and women in Congress how much of a threat U.S. antinarcotics policy is to personal security in Mexico, or how thoroughly Mexicans detest the U.S. fence.

This book is being written at a time of severe stress in the global financial system, and the exact nature of the changes that will take place over the next few years is impossible to predict. Mexican authorities have sought for many years to strengthen their country's finances to insulate Mexico from developments in the United States. The hope was that Mexico could decouple itself sufficiently so that when the United States experienced financial or economic difficulties, these did not automatically translate into major problems in Mexico. Mexico ran fiscal surpluses, kept inflation low, built up foreign reserves, controlled its foreign borrowing, allowed foreign banks to dominate the banking sector, and kept the current account deficits in the balance of payments low. Despite all these accomplishments, it has become clear that Mexico is not decoupled from the United States. Trade credit is scarce, and the peso has depreciated, raising the cost of imported goods and servicing foreign debt.

Mexico and the United States are still attached at the hip. This is deeply understood by Mexican officials, but the reality is only vaguely grasped by U.S. authorities. This is one difference in the thinking of a dependent nation compared with its dominant partner.

Notes

Prologue

1. IMF, "Mexico 2007 Article IV Consultation." Purchasing power parity (PPP) seeks to measure purchasing power across countries.

2. This prologue is not intended to be a history of Mexico. Rather, one way of demonstrating the importance of Juárez is to cite one of Mexico's outstanding current historians, Enrique Krauze. Krauze (*Mexico, Biography of Power,* 202) wrote: "During the age of the caudillos and the *criollos,* Mexico was not a nation. It was an aggregate of regions and localities without national consciousness. . . . When Juárez died . . . Mexico had become a locus of history and reality." Ibid.

3. The scholar Francisco Gonzalez, in *Dual Transitions from Authoritarian Rule,* has argued that the success in both Mexico and Chile compared with other regional countries lay in their highly institutionalized authoritarian regimes and not in authoritarian rule per se. The argument is that the institutional aspect of the PRI lent itself to a successful transition.

4. I refer here to gerrymandering of congressional districts in the United States and the role that money plays in U.S. elections. Nothing in Mexico's procedural decisions about which I am aware is as questionable as the arbitrary decisions, including that of the U.S. Supreme Court, that put George W. Bush in the White House in 2000. Andrés Manuel López Obrador of the Party of the Democratic Revolution (Partido de la Revolución Democrática, PDR), who lost an extremely close presidential election in 2006, complained bitterly at the time that the vote count was rigged against him, but the investigative procedures were extensive and apparently less arbitrary than in the U.S. presidential election of 2000.

5. World Bank, *World Development Indicators,* 1982–2007 data.

6. Ibid., 2004 data (the most recently reported data for income share held by top 10 percent and income share held by bottom 20 percent).

7. Levy, *Progress against Poverty.*

8. Data combined from the U.S. Census Bureau, Foreign Trade Division, *Related Party Trade, 2007*; and World Bank, *World Development Indicators, 2007* data.

Chapter 1. Introduction: Mexico's Political Economy

Epigraphs: Octavio Paz, *The New Yorker,* September 17, 1979; Will Rogers, Will Rogers Memorial Museum, "More Letters from a Self-Made Diplomat to His President," *Saturday Evening Post,* May 12, 1928.

1. This was not the only reason for Aguilar Zinser's dismissal, however; there were important philosophical differences between him and the Mexican foreign minister, Luis Ernesto Derbez. The words Aguilar Zinser used in Spanish were "patio trasero."

2. Meyer and Sherman, *Course of Mexican History*, 531–34.

3. Andrew Selee, head of the Mexico Program at the Woodrow Wilson Center for Scholars, made this point in a 2007 pamphlet, "More Than Neighbors."

4. Paz, "Reflections: Mexico and the United States," 136. Paz's most famous book, certainly for U.S. readers, is *The Labyrinth of Solitude*.

5. Paz, "Reflections: Mexico and the United States," 148.

6. Ibid, 153.

7. González et al., *Global Views 2004*. This publication was supported by CIDE, COMEXI, and the Chicago Council on Foreign Relations.

8. CIDE and COMEXI, "Mexico and the World 2006."

9. BBC World Service, "World View of U.S. Role Goes from Bad to Worse," January 23, 2007, available online at http://news.bbc.co.uk/2/shared/bsp/hi/pdfs/23_01_07_us_poll.pdf.

10. Castañeda, in *ExMex*, gives an account of the context in which this statement was made as well as a personal justification for his position.

11. The freelance journalist Dolia Estévez, who has lived in the United States for many years, wrote a brief but thorough account of this incident in "¿Oportunidad desperdiciada?" in the Mexican journal *Poder y negocios*, dated June 17, 2008.

12. Serrano, "Bordering on the Impossible."

13. Ortiz Mena, "Getting to 'No.'"

14. Odell, "Latin American Trade Negotiations with the United States."

15. Habeeb, *Power and Tactics in International Negotiation*.

16. Zartman, "Structuralist Dilemma in Negotiation."

17. Data in this paragraph is from World Bank, *World Development Indicators*, 1982–2008 data.

18. "Mexico's Mezzogiorno," *Economist* (November 2006): 7–9.

19. Although Calderón delivered all the fact-filled papers to the congress to back up the statements in his Informe on September 1, the usual date for this address, representatives of the PRD blocked his access to the chambers because Andrés Manuel López Obrador was still contesting the validity of his defeat. The speech itself was made from the National Palace on the next day.

20. Brazil collects about 35 percent of GDP in taxes, high by Latin American standards. The norm for the region is around 17 percent.

21. The government in recent years has been able to allocate some funds back to Pemex because of high oil prices, but most of the government's extra revenue was used for other purposes, such as to subsidize gasoline prices in Mexico. These subsidies in 2008 amounted to some US$19 billion, a substantial figure.

22. IMF, "Mexico 2007 Article IV Consultation."

23. Fernando Turner, businessman and officer of ANEI, interview with the author, November 3, 2007, Monterrey, Mexico.

24. The source for most of the material in this paragraph is Estévez, "¿Oportunidad desperdiciada?"

25. Sergio Sarmiento, a regular columnist in the Mexico City daily newspaper *Reforma* and the host of a popular radio talk show, had a column that dealt with this subject: "Campo y pobreza," *Reforma*, January 14, 2006.

26. Stevern Zahniser and William Coyle, "U.S.-Mexico Corn Trade during the NAFTA Era: New Twists to an Old Story," Economic Research Service, U.S. Department of Agriculture, May 2004.

27. Levy, *Progress against Poverty.*

28. IMF, "Mexico 2007 Article IV Consultation."

29. OECD, *Latin American Economic Outlook.*

30. Embassy of Mexico, "Judicial and Public Safety Reform."

31. Agren, "Drugs, Energy, Economy Beset Mexico's Calderón in Second Year." A version of this article was published in the *Mexico City News* on July 16, 2008.

32. Olson, *Rise and Decline of Nations.*

33. Baylis and Perloff, "End Runs around Trade Restrictions."

34. Javier Treviño, conversation with the author, November 16, 2007. Treviño is senior vice president of corporate communication and public affairs of Cemex.

35. James Jones, interview with the author, June 12, 2008, Washington, D.C.

Chapter 2. Trade: From Closure to Opening

Epigraphs: Salinas de Gortari, *México, un paso difícil a la modernidad*, 52; Adam Smith, *The Wealth of Nations* (New York: Random House, 1937), 461.

1. This history is discussed briefly in Meyer and Sherman, *Course of Mexican History*, 593–94.

2. Data from IMF, International Financial Statistics Database.

3. I had many informal conversations with Prebisch over the years on this point. I admired his acuity and conviction, but I thought he had a fixation on his own CEPAL model.

4. During the mid-1960s, when I was in charge of the commercial policy unit in the U.S. State Department, I was asked because of my position and my ability to speak and understand Spanish to lead periodic bilateral trade talks with Mexico. The chief Mexican delegate in his opening remarks read a long, prepared statement to the effect that as a developing country, Mexico should be given trade privileges in the U.S. market but, of course, could not provide any reciprocity. This could hardly be called a negotiation, and I said as much. At our next meeting the opening comments of the Mexican delegate were more or less the same as at the previous meeting. I stopped going to the meetings and assigned a more junior officer to this task.

5. Bueno, "La estructura de la protección efectiva en México." The article was published in English as Gerardo M. Bueno, "The Structure of Protection in Mexico," in Balassa, *Structure of Protection in Developing Countries.*

6. Juan Carlos Baker, "TLCAN: 12 años de libre comercio" (NAFTA: Twelve

years of trade), Secretaría de Economía, director de evaluación y seguimiento de negociaciones, Mexico City, May 2, 2006.

7. Vega Cánovas, "De la protección a la apertura comercial."

8. Ibid.

9. Baker, "TLCAN: 12 años de libre comercio."

10. Schettino, *Cien años de confusión,* 14.

11. Salinas de Gortari, *México, un paso difícil a la modernidad.*

12. Interestingly, this is the same way that Canada started before it realized that free trade required a full-blown free trade agreement.

13. John Negroponte, conversation with the author, Washington, D.C., June 12, 2008.

14. The Canada–U.S. free trade agreement (CUSFTA) represented a major departure in U.S. trade policy because it was the first big shift away from U.S. adherence to nondiscrimination in international trade—"most-favored-nation" trade treatment, in more technical parlance. The United States had concluded an FTA with Israel that had entered into force on August 19, 1985, but this was seen largely as a political agreement, whereas CUSFTA was between the United States and its most important trade partner.

15. On a personal note, I wrote a book published by the Brookings Institution in 1984 entitled *Free Trade between Mexico and the United States?* which was prompted by my conviction that Mexico's pre-1982 development policy would give way and that the most logical alternative was to seek better access to the U.S. market. The few reviews that it received argued that I did not understand Mexican antipathy to having closer political and economic relations with the United States. I thought at the time that it would take about twenty years for bilateral free trade to become a reality, but it took only about ten.

16. Mayer, *Interpreting NAFTA,* contains an excellent treatment of the negotiation.

17. Thomas F. "Mack" McLarty recalled that peanuts and sugar had to be removed after they had been included in the negotiations to secure enough votes to pass the enabling legislation for NAFTA (Thomas McLarty, interview with the author, Washington, D.C., May 27, 2008). The removal of sugar took place in what was purported to be an exchange of letters between the two chief negotiators, Mickey Kantor on the U.S. side and Jaime Serra on the Mexican side. The problem was that the Mexican side never formally agreed in writing to the Kantor letter removing sugar. This led to later disputes when the Mexican side imposed antidumping duties on high fructose corn syrup from the United States, used mainly to sweeten soft drinks, although in reality this was retaliation for the U.S. action on sugar. The sugar issue has since been resolved.

18. Hufbauer and Schott, *North American Free Trade,* and *NAFTA: An Assessment* are two of the publications written at the time of the negotiations.

19. What follows, unless otherwise indicated, are my opinions.

20. Figures are from Mexico's ministry of economy, with data from the Banco de México.

21. Data from the Banco de México and Mexico's ministry of the economy.

22. Wise, "Unfulfilled Promise," 39.

23. Watkins, "China Challenge."

24. Ibid.

25. Wise, "Unfulfilled Promise," 28

26. Papademetriou et al., "NAFTA's Promise and Reality."

27. Weintraub, "Scoring Free Trade."

28. Von Bertrab, *Negotiating NAFTA*. The original Spanish publication in 1996 was entitled *El redescubrimiento de América: Historia del TLC* (Mexico City: Fondo de Cultura Económica).

29. See Weintraub, *NAFTA's Impact on North America*.

30. Morales Moreno, *Post-NAFTA North America*.

31. Anderson and Sands, "Negotiating North America."

32. Pastor's most recent commentary is "Future of North America."

33. CFR, "Building a North American Community."

34. Schott, "Trade Negotiations among NAFTA Partners." For the benefit of readers who do not closely follow trade issues, an FTA needs rules of origin to prevent shipment by a nonmember of the group to a member with a low tariff for transshipment to a member with a higher tariff. The rules are designed to identify products that originate in the member countries, taking into account that products often have imported inputs. These rules of origin are often used as subterfuge for protectionism, as was the case in the automotive and textile sectors of NAFTA. A country that is a member of a customs union, with a common external tariff, cannot normally join an FTA that gives duty-free treatment to a nonmember because this would violate the common external tariff. The European Union (EU) has many FTAs with nonmembers, but with the EU as a whole and not just with particular members. Mexico, for example, has an FTA with the EU and could not technically maintain this if it became part of a North American customs union.

35. Rubio, "NAFTA and Mexico." Rubio is one of Mexico's most respected commentators.

Chapter 3. Foreign Direct Investment and Finance: From Resistance to Welcome

Epigraphs: Bruno Ferrari, the head of ProMexico, the government agency promoting investment, quoted in Stephen Fidler, "Hesitant Steps over Reform Hinder Growth," *Financial Times*, special report: "Mexico—Trade & Investment," November 17, 2008, 1; OECD, *Economic Survey*, 2007.

1. President José López Portillo, Informe Presidencial (State of the Union Address), September 1, 1982. See also Soledad Loaeza, *Las consequencias políticas de la expropriación bancaria* (Mexico City: El Colegio de México, 2008).

2. I know this because I was in Mexico during this time, and all the informed speculation of the experts with whom I spoke was just how much payment above book value would be obtained.

3. "FOBAPROA: Paso a Paso," citing "La política económica en México, 1950–1994," available online at http://diputados.gob.mx/cronica57/contenido/cont2/fobapro1.htm.

4. Haber, "Mexico's Experiments with Bank Privatization and Liberalization, 1991–2003," draft of October 18, mimeo. Other information in this paragraph comes from the same source.

5. Haber (ibid.) cites a particular well-documented case in which a group of purchasers financed 75 percent of the cost of acquiring a bank by loans from the bank being purchased and then using these shares as collateral for the loan.

6. Ibid.

7. Weintraub, *Financial Decision-making in Mexico,* 35–38 and 58.

8. An account of these developments can be found in ibid.

9. Ibid., 139. Other material in this paragraph comes from this same source.

10. I was marginally involved in this legislative effort. The Senate Foreign Relations Committee, then under the chairmanship of Senator Jesse Helms, held a hearing on January 26, 1995, on the loan guaranty legislation. The hearing had been stacked with three opponents of the legislation. Because I favored the loan guaranty, I was urged to testify by the Democratic staff of the committee. The other three witnesses were Malcom (Steve) Forbes Jr., editor of *Forbes Magazine*; William Seidman, a former head of the Federal Deposit Insurance Corporation; and Larry Kudlow, a financial expert.

11. Opponents of the arrangements used this argument for the sale in 2008 of the Bear Stearns investment banking company facilitated by the U.S. Treasury and Federal Reserve Bank of New York.

12. Weintraub, *Financial Decision-making in Mexico,* 142.

13. Hufbauer and Schott, *NAFTA: An Assessment,* 61–62.

14. Most of what follows in the next three paragraphs comes from two sources: Mackey, "Report of Michael W. Mackey"; and McQuerry, "Banking Sector Rescue in Mexico."

15. McQuerry, "Banking Sector Rescue in Mexico."

16. Most of this information is from ibid.

17. I spent much time in Mexico during the 1990s. Just about all middle-class people with whom I spoke were distressed about financial problems they faced starting in 1995, and they put much of the blame for their problems on the activities of the reprivatized banks. Unless they were dedicated *priistas*, they supported the opposition in the 1997 congressional elections and in the 2000 presidential election, when the PRI was voted out of office.

18. The data come from, both from the World Bank, Thorsten Beck and Maria Soledad Martinez Peria, "Foreign Bank Acquisitions and Outreach, Evidence from Mexico," drafted for the IMF discussion "On the Causes and Consequences of Structural Reforms," ideas presented from many major capitals to IMF headquarters in Washington, D.C., February 28–29, 2008. The authors are both from the World Bank.

19. Ibid.

20. IMF, "Mexico 2007 Article IV Consultation."

21. Lowe, "Direct Investment, 2004–2007."

22. Hufbauer and Schott, *NAFTA: An Assessment*, 79–84.

Chapter 4. Narcotics: Effect of Profits from U.S. Consumption

Epigraphs: President Ernesto Zedillo, UN Global Drug Summit, New York, June 8, 1998; "U.S. National Drug Control Strategy, 2008 Annual Report," statement by John P. Walters, director of the White House Office of National Drug Control Policy, Washington, D.C., 2008.

1. A February 23, 2006, letter under the name of Walter Cronkite on behalf of the Drug Policy Alliance states flat out that the "war on drugs is a failure." The justification for this statement is that drug use in the United States has been hardly affected despite the expenditure of hundreds of billions of dollars, locking up millions of people, and tapping telephones. Ethan Nadelman, who has examined this subject for many years, wrote a brief comment in *Foreign Policy*, "Addicted to Failure: It's Time for Latin America to Start Breaking with Washington over the War on Drugs," (July–August 2003): 94–95.

2. Davidow, *Bear and the Porcupine*, 238.

3. María Celia Toro, "Mexican Policy against Drugs: From Deterring to Embracing the United States," in Weintraub, *NAFTA's Impact on North America*, 209–34.

4. The drug certification process involved other countries in addition to Mexico.

5. Kleiman, "Dopey, Boozy, Smoky—and Stupid."

6. Grossman, Chaloupka, and Shim, "Illegal Drug Use and Public Policy."

7. Becker, Murphy, and Grossman, "Market for Illegal Goods." Gary S. Becker is a Nobel Laureate in economics.

8. Printed in the January 8, 2008, edition of the newspaper.

9. Grossman, Chaloupka, and Shim, "Illegal Drug Use and Public Policy."

10. According to the National Drug Intelligence Center's "National Drug Threat Assessment 2008," published in October 2007, drug-related arrests were lower in 2006 than in the previous three years. Much of the information in this paragraph comes from this source.

11. Caulkins and Reuter, "Revisiting U.S. Drug Policy."

12. Alexander Higgins, "Swiss Approve Pioneering Legal Heroin Program," Associated Press, November 30, 2008. The heroin is produced by a government-approved laboratory and serves nearly thirteen hundred selected addicts twice a day. By contrast, however, a program to decriminalize the use of marijuana was rejected; the Swiss government opposed the marijuana program because it would cause problems with neighboring countries.

13. Califano, "Should Drugs Be Decriminalized?" 967.

14. Roumasset and Thaw, "Economics of Prohibition."

15. Becker, Murphy, and Grossman, "Market for Illegal Goods."

16. "Zogby Interactive Likely Voters 9/23/08 thru 9/25/08 MOE +/- 1.5 percentage

points," *Zogby International,* September 25, 2008, shows only 8.2 percent of those polled favor "ending the war on drugs." I find the question faulty, however; it should have asked respondents if they favored "decriminalizing" the use of narcotics.

17. Chabat, "Mexico's War on Drugs."

18. Astorga, "Drug Trafficking in Mexico."

19. Reuter and Ronfeldt, "Quest for Integrity." This was the Mexican view not only in the 1980s, but even more so in the 1960s and 1970s.

20. John Ehrlichman, then a senior adviser to President Nixon, wrote in the report of the task force overseeing this operation that "the task force recommends that the Mexican government be forced into a program of defoliation of marijuana plants (using borrowed or leased equipment from the United States) by commencing a program of strict enforcement and customs inspection at the border." See Special Presidential Task Force Relating to Narcotics, Marihuana, and Dangerous Drugs.

21. Celia Toro, *Mexico's War on Drugs,* 1.

22. Chabat, "La militarización de la lucha contra el narcotráfico."

23. Roig-Franzia, "Drug Trade Tyranny on the Border."

24. Cook, "Mexico's Drug Cartels."

25. These facts were publicized in a release by the Mexican embassy in the United States in May 2008.

26. Grayson, "Los Zetas."

27. "Five Killed in Mexico Border City amid Drug War."

28. CPJ, *Attacks on the Press in 2007,* 90–93.

29. I was present at a meeting on April 3, 2008, at the Woodrow Wilson International Center for Scholars put on in cooperation with the Committee to Protect Journalists at which three working Mexican journalists discussed their experiences in reporting drug-related crimes. They corroborated the point that many Mexican newspapers and television stations are not investigating drug-related crimes. They noted that manuals have been published to provide guidance to reporters on self-protection when they look into these crimes. They also confirmed that when articles were published on these crimes, they were usually left unsigned.

30. Cook, "Mexico's Drug Cartels"; Grayson, "Los Zetas"; and Strategic Forecasting, Inc. (more commonly known as Stratfor), "Mexican Drug Cartels: Government Progress and Growing Violence," Austin, Tex., December 11, 2008.

31. I spent two months in Mexico working on this book during the summer of 2008, and stories on violence and impunity were on page one of newspapers and on television every day.

32. Chabat, "Mexico," 28.

33. Farkus, in "Mexico Wages Bloody War with Drug Cartels," refers to this statement made by George Friedman, who heads a private intelligence group in Texas. Also available online at http://www.VOANEWS.com/English/2008-05-21-voa76.cfm.

34. Corchado, "Drug Czar Says U.S. Use Fueling Mexican Violence."

35. Kleiman, "Dopey, Boozy, Smoky—and Stupid."

36. Chabat, "Mexico's War on Drugs."

37. Verini, "Arming the Drug Wars." The article describes how the weapons are

purchased. The author asserts that "buying guns in America is easy. Transporting them across the border requires more invention."

38. Peter DeShazo and Johanna Mendelson Forman, "Making the Most of Mérida," Americas Program, Center for Strategic and International Studies, August 2008. This piece was also published as an op-ed article, "Sacar provecho al Plan Mérida," in the Mexican newspaper *El universal.*

39. Storrs, "Mexico's Counter-Narcotics Efforts under Fox," 14.

40. DeYoung, "Mexican Envoy Highly Critical of U.S. Role in Anti-Drug Effort." The *Washington Post* interviewer was Karen DeYoung.

41. "Mexico and the United States: A Wary Friendship," with the subheading: "Amid bad temper and wounded pride, Mexico and the United States inch towards compromise on a plan to boost the fight against drug crime."

42. Fuentes, "Pone EU auditor al Plan Mérida."

43. An interesting example of these notices was issued on April 30, 2009, when the Mexican embassy in Washington, D.C., announced that "Mexican police detained suspected Zeta gang leader Gregorio Sauceda Gamboa, aka 'el Goyo' in the border city of Matamoros" the day before.

44. Celia Toro, *Mexico's War on Drugs.*

45. Harman, "Lawmakers Vowed Monday to Pass a Bill." The mayors of U.S. border cities were concerned about drug tourism, and Washington, D.C., added the contention that the bill would increase drug consumption.

46. Davidow, as quoted in Roig-Franzia, "Anti-Drug Assistance Approved for Mexico."

Chapter 5. Energy: The Oil Is Ours

Epigraphs: Mexican Secretariat of Energy and Petróleos Mexicanos, *Diagnosis: Situation of Pemex* (Mexico City, 2007); Sarah O. Ladislaw, "Outlook for Energy," in *The Future of North America, 2025,* edited by Armand B. Peschard-Sverdrup, 1–37 (Washington, D.C.: CSIS Press), 11.

1. On North Korea see Brooke, "Tentatively, North Korea Solicits Foreign Investment and Tourism."

2. Latin America and the Caribbean are replete with NOCs; the two big exceptions are Canada and the United States.

3. An important poll on this and other foreign policy issues was conducted by CIDE and COMEXI, "Mexico and the World 2006." The findings were that 76 percent of the public was against allowing foreigners to invest in oil, while 62 percent of leaders favored allowing foreigners to invest in oil.

4. David Luhnow, "Mexico Tries to Save a Big, Fading Oil Field," *Wall Street Journal,* April 4, 2007, 1, provides useful background on Cantarell and how it was discovered by accident by a fisherman, after whom the field was named.

5. Mexican Secretariat of Energy and Petróleos Mexicanos, *Diagnosis: Situation of Pemex,* 9. *Reforma,* August 22, 2008, contains data on the decline of crude oil production during the first seven months of 2008.

6. Jiménez, "Cae 18% exportación de crudo."

7. Calculating the amount of proven reserves is not a precise exercise. A few years before Pemex circulated its March 20, 2009, figures, the Mexico's Secretariat of Energy (Secretaría de Energía, SENER), in a 2007 report titled "Perspectiva de Mercado de Petróleo Crudo 2007–2016," gave a lower figure of 11 billion barrels of proven oil reserves for 2007. The current Pemex advisory states that proven oil reserves as of January 1, 2007, were 15.5 billion barrels. Pemex estimates that 61 percent of 2009 proven reserves are heavy oil, 31 percent light, and 8 percent extra light.

8. Sidney Weintraub and Rafael Fernández de Castro, "Mexico," in Weintraub, Hester, and Prado, *Energy Cooperation in the Western Hemisphere*, 106–31.

9. The peak price for Mexican oil in the world market was $131 a barrel in July 2008, when the West Texas Intermediate price reached $147 a barrel; the Mexican oil mixture sold at an average price of $97.90 a barrel from January through July of 2008.

10. An informative commentary on this subject appeared in an op-ed column by Rogelio Ramírez de la O, "Petroleo, oportunidad perdida," in *El universal* on July 23, 2008.

11. Lajous's article, "La propiedad de los hidrocarburos," was sent to me by e-mail. It was later published in mid-2007 in *El mundo del petróleo*.

12. Guerrero, "Exige IP reformar PEMEX . . . y sindicato." "IP" refers to the private sector.

13. Crooks and Thomson, "Setback for Mexico."

14. In Weintraub and Fernández de Castro, "Mexico," a map on page 122 illustrates precisely this.

15. Jank et al., "E.U. and U.S. Policies on Biofuels," is an excellent discussion of the various ways in which ethanol is produced.

16. The specifics on the proposal come from a handout on Calderón's presentation to the Mexican congress.

17. Córdoba, "Reprueba PEMEX propuesta priista."

18. Rubio, "Sacralización."

19. Verrastro, "United States."

20. Two of the most widely read private studies are Council on Foreign Relations, *National Security Consequences of U.S. Oil Dependency*, by John Deutch and James R. Schlesinger (chairs) and David G. Victor (director); and that of the U.S. National Petroleum Council, "Facing the Hard Truths about Energy: A Comprehensive View to 2030 of Oil and Natural Gas."

21. Council on Foreign Relations, *National Security Consequences of U.S. Oil Dependency*, 14.

22. Jank et al., "E.U. and U.S. Policies on Biofuels." The U.S. most-favored-nation customs duty, which is the one that applies to Brazil, is 2.5 percent; in addition, there is a secondary tariff of 14 cents a liter, or an ad valorem equivalent of 46 percent.

23. Wolf, "Welcome to the New World," 11.

24. For a good article on this subject, see Elizabeth Kolbert, "Unconventional Crude: Canada's Synthetic Fuels Boom," *The New Yorker*, November 12, 2007, 46–51.

25. Section 526 of the U.S. Energy Independence and Security Act reads as follows:

"No Federal agency shall enter into a contract for procurement of an alternative or synthetic fuel, including a fuel produced from nonconventional petroleum sources, for any mobility-related use, other than for research or testing, unless the contract specifies that the lifecycle greenhouse gas emissions associated with the production and combustion of the fuel supplied under the contract must, on an ongoing basis, be less than or equal to such emissions from the equivalent conventional fuel produced from conventional petroleum sources."

26. Gudynas, "Energy Diplomacy and the Crossroads in South American Unification." The lack of energy cooperation in the Western Hemisphere is the central theme of Weintraub, Hester, and Prado, *Energy Cooperation in the Western Hemisphere*.

27. Lajous, "Política petrolera exterior."

28. Angel Vela, "Importa PEMEX 50% de gasolina." The quantities cited in the article were 404,000 barrels a day of gasoline imported out of 809,000 barrels a day sold in the country.

29. Jardón, "Costarán subsidios a energéticos más de 340 mil milliones de pesos."

30. Two excellent U.S. accounts of this incident are George W. Grayson, "Mexico and the United States: The Natural Gas Controversy," in *The Politics of Mexican Oil*, edited by George W. Grayson, 183–202 (Pittsburgh, Pa.: University of Pittsburgh Press, 1980); and Joseph M. Dukert, "How an Earlier Effort Foundered," chapter 6 of Dukert's "Creation and Evolution of North America's Gas and Electricity Regime: A Dynamic Example of Interdependence," Ph.D. dissertation, School for Advanced International Studies, Johns Hopkins University, 2004.

31. Ortiz Mena, "Getting to 'No.'"

Chapter 6. Migration: A Consequence of Inequality

Epigraphs: Ray Marshall, the former U.S. secretary of labor, "Getting Immigration Reform Right," Economic Policy Institute briefing paper, March 15, 2007, 5; Jorge G. Castañeda, the former Mexican foreign minister, "Call off the Immigration Hunt," *New York Times*, December 28, 2008, WK9.

1. Lindsay, Perderzini, and Passel, "Demography of Mexico/U.S. Migration."

2. Roberts, "Special Report on Migration," 6. The German data are from 2003.

3. Rivero and Carrillo, "Tienen mas trabajo . . . ¡en EU!"

4. Alba, "Mexican Economy and Mexico-U.S. Migration."

5. I was a proponent of integration, and I expected economic convergence between Mexico and the United States to take place. Ireland, because of its high growth in GDP, was referred to as a "Celtic tiger" for many years after it became a member of the European Union, but its economic collapse in 2009 has been more severe than in other EU countries as a consequence of the global financial crisis. Spain, which also grew rapidly after it joined the EU, is now facing low growth and rising unemployment.

6. I wrote the first draft of this chapter in Cuernavaca, in the Mexican state of Morelos, when primary and secondary school teachers were on strike. One demand of the teachers was to retain the right of inheritance of teaching jobs, or, if there is no heir, the ability to sell the teaching right. I later learned that this provision on the sale of

teaching positions is widespread in union contracts with the authorities. See Puryear, "Reform in Mexico Forces Debate."

7. My view is that the bilateral migration issue could be better managed than is being done today, but without economic growth this just manages how the migration flow takes place without really affecting the emigration incentive.

8. Mexican Ministry of Foreign Affairs and U.S. Commission on Immigration Reform, *Migration between Mexico and the United States*, 448.

9. These were (1) quantification of the migration between the two countries, (2) characteristics of the Mexican migrants in the United States, (3) factors that influence migration, (4) impacts of the migration in the two countries, and (5) responses to the migration.

10. Figures are from the Inter-American Development Bank, augmented by estimates from Banamex.

11. E-mail to the author, April 30, 2008, from Carlos Villanueva, president of the Worldwide Association of Mexicans Abroad.

12. There are good discussions of U.S. border enforcement efforts in Deborah W. Meyers, "U.S. Border Enforcement: From Horseback to High-Tech," Migration Policy Institute (MPI), *Insight* no. 7 (November 2005): 1–31; and Meyers, "One Face at the Border."

13. I have previously written on this subject. See Sidney Weintraub, "Confused and Mean-Spirited U.S. Handling of Immigration Problems," *Issues in International Political Economy*, no. 102 (June 2008). I have been writing *Issues* commentaries monthly for almost nine years and distributing them by e-mail.

14. Preston, "270 Immigrants Sent to Prison in Federal Push." In a second article, "An Interpreter Speaking Up for Migrants," Preston reported that the interpreter for the earlier proceedings in Waterloo, Iowa, Professor Camayd-Freixas, had written an essay saying he was taken aback by the rapid pace of the proceedings and the pressure brought to bear on the defendants, most of whom could not read or write.

15. This was during a joint press conference with the secretary of commerce, Carlos Gutierrez, on June 9, 2008. Barack Obama, in his acceptance speech as the Democratic nominee for president of the United States said that, if elected, he would look into the problem of family separation.

16. Camerota, "Immigrants in the United States, 2007."

17. "Migrantes Mexicanos fallecidos en la frontera sur de EUA en su intento por internarse sin documentos (por estado)," communication from the Mexican Embassy in Washington, D.C., based on data compiled in Mexico in early 2008.

18. Castañeda, quoted in Pantin, "Se deshizo lo andado."

19. Castañeda, *ExMex: From Migrants to Immigrants*. Castañeda also says that Mexico reacted too slowly to the 9/11 attacks and that may have contributed to the indefinite postponement of the immigration negotiations (page 93).

20. Fox and Allyn, *Revolution of Hope*, 28.

21. Roig-Franzia, "Mexican Leader Sees Bias."

22. Fox and Allyn, *Revolution of Hope*, xviii.

23. Weintraub, "Development Aid Can Ease Illegal Immigration."

24. Martin, *Importing Poverty?*, devotes much attention to technical innovation in harvesting fruit and vegetable crops that now rely heavily on hand labor.

Chapter 7. The Border: A Phenomenon of Its Own

Epigraphs: Manuel Suárez-Mier, of the Mexican embassy in the United States, "A View from the South," *Foreign Service Journal* (October 2007): 17–22, quotation on 22; Stephen Flynn, "Beyond Border Control," 58.

1. This data comes from Elise Labott, "Analysis: Clinton Taking U.S.-Mexico Relations beyond Drug War," *CNN.com*, March 24, 2009, available online at http://www.cnn.com/2009/POLITICS/03/24/us.mexico/.

2. Barbara Kotschwar, "Bumps in the Road to NAFTA Implementation," Peterson Institute for International Economics, Washington, D.C., 2008.

3. Camerota, "Immigrants in the United States, 2007," published by the Center for Immigration Studies (CIS). The CIS bias is anti-immigrant, but the figures in this estimate jibe with calculations made by other experts with different biases.

4. The Mexico-U.S. border runs for almost two thousand miles. It is made up of four U.S. states (Arizona, California, New Mexico, and Texas) and six Mexican states (Baja California Norte, Chihuahua, Coahuila, Nuevo León, Sonora, and Tamaulipas).

5. Ismael Aguilar Barajas, "Frontera norte de México: Agenda de desarrollo e integración económica. Reflexiones sobre el Noreste de México-Texas," *Revista mexicana de política exterior*, no. 81 (October 2007): 125–55. The growth in northern Mexico since NAFTA had the adverse effect of increasing the income disparity between that region and the poorer states in southern Mexico.

6. U.S. Department of Homeland Security and Mexico's Secretaría of Gobernación, "Mexico-U.S. Border Partnership."

7. The data come from El Colegio de la Frontera Norte, "U.S.-Mexico Ports of Entry: A Capacity Analysis and Recommendations for Increased Efficiency," Tijuana, December 19, 2007. The data were compiled from a northbound sample of fifty-two hundred pedestrian crossers and sixty-four hundred drivers of passenger vehicles. The times given are estimates.

8. Ibid., based on a sample of four thousand freight transporters. These figures are estimates. Making estimates on the time for truck passage is particularly difficult because of the need to transfer the cargo to a U.S. truck in a U.S. federal compound after it is inspected by Mexican authorities.

9. Alejandro Ibarra-Yúnez, "Secure Borders and Free Trade: An Institutional Economics Approach," mimeograph, 2007. This article is available in Spanish as well: Ibarra-Yúnez, "Fronteras seguras y facilitación de comercio."

10. Alden, *Closing of the American Border.*

11. Flynn, "False Conundrum."

12. There is a similar effort to move many U.S.-Canada activities away from the border. There has been little trilateralism so far in extraborder measures, although there may be scope for this in the future.

13. Flynn, "Beyond Border Control."

14. Hufbauer and Vega Cánovas, "Whither NAFTA."

15. U.S. Customs and Border Protection, online at http://www.customs.gov/xp/cgov/home.xml.

16. CFR, *Building a North American Community.*

17. Anderson and Sands, *Negotiating North America.*

18. Biersteker, "Rebordering of North America."

19. Martin, "Embracing Change on the U.S.-Mexico Border." This issue of the *Foreign Service Journal* contains a number of articles on the U.S. borders with Mexico and Canada.

20. Villa, "Transaction Costs in the Transportation Sector and Infrastructure in North America," 31–32.

21. Ibid., 23–25.

22. NASTC, "Border Story."

23. What is said here about Mexico-U.S. trade also applies to Canadian trade within North America; the discussion here is confined to the United States and Mexico.

24. Another reason for this diminution is that the system of product and country quotas for textile and clothing exports to the United States was terminated.

25. These figures come from research on trucking by Barbara Kotschwar of the Peterson Institute for International Economics and Georgetown University (see her article "Bumps in the Road to NAFTA Implementation"). Much of the information in the following paragraphs was provided to me by this same source.

26. FMCSA, *NAFTA Safety Statistics Database.* Once, when I was crossing from Mexico into the United States by car, I saw advertisements on the border soliciting Mexican truck drivers to apply for work with U.S. companies. I took this to mean that at least some U.S. companies did not believe the arguments put forth by the Teamsters Union. There would be considerable benefits for Mexican truck drivers to shift from Mexican to U.S. companies, in terms of higher salaries and better infrastructure at truck stops for eating and sleeping. The Monterrey, Mexico, newspaper *El norte* had a supplement called "Transporte" in November 2007 that contains much information about companies that have trucking operations in both Mexico and the United States and on the lack of what it called *"paraderos dignos"* ("dignified truck stops") in Mexico.

27. Villa, "Border Transportation Studies Review."

28. This information was provided to me in an e-mail from Juan Carlos Villa, February 7, 2008.

29. My career in the government involved much work on trade policy, and my outlook was that the United States took seriously the trade commitments it made. Trade actions taken by the United States have been overturned by dispute-settlement panels and in trade litigation, but there typically has been an arguable basis for any given action taken by the United States. This is not so for the trucking actions regarding Mexico. They have been conscious and repeated violations of formal agreements entered into by the United States. I have asked colleagues if they can point to other cases of deliberate refusal to carry out commitments entered into in trade agreements. I

have heard none and would appreciate hearing from readers who can cite other similar cases.

30. See Sidney Weintraub, "Mexico Is Right to Retaliate on Trade," *Forbes.com*, Available online at http://www.forbes.com/2009/03/19/us-mexico-trade-opinions-contributors-trucks.html.

31. Skerry, "How Not to Build a Fence," has pictures of the appearance of the fence at different points.

32. Egan, "Disorder on the Border." For example, Egan's op-ed quotes Governor Janet Napolitano of Arizona: "Show me a 50-foot wall and I'll show you a 51-foot ladder."

33. Roig-Franzia, "Apparent Mexican Winner Attacks Border Wall."

34. "Good Neighbors Make Fences," 25–27. The quotations shown are in the original text.

35. Flynn, "False Conundrum."

Chapter 8. Findings: Changing Traditional Practiceso

1. Celia Toro, *Mexico's War on Drugs*, 1.

2. Muñoz, *Solitary War*, provides much detail on the U.S pressure.

3. The United States, however, has paid little heed to efficiency in its trucking arrangements with Canada by allowing cabotage—i.e., permitting trucks that bring cargo directly to U.S. destinations to carry cargo to other U.S. destinations before returning to Canada.

4. Santiago Levy, *Good Intentions, Bad Outcomes: Social Policy, Informality, and Economic Growth in Mexico* (Washington, D.C.: Brookings Institution, 2008) deals with the latter problem, specifically the unequal social benefits of workers with similar characteristics.

5. Robert Pastor has made this suggestion in *Toward a North American Community: Lessons from the Old World for the New* (Washington, D.C.: Peterson Institute, 2001).

Bibliography

Agren, David. "Drugs, Energy, Economy Beset Mexico's Calderón in Second Year." *World Politics Review*, July 16, 2008.

Alba, Francisco. "The Mexican Economy and Mexico–U.S. Migration." In *Mexico–U.S. Migration Management: A Binational Approach*. Edited by Susan F. Martin and Agustin Escobar Latapi. New York: Lexington Books, 2008.

Alden, Edward. *The Closing of the American Border: Terrorism, Immigration, and Security since 9/11*. New York: Harper, 2008.

Anderson, Greg, and Christopher Sands. *Negotiating North America: The Security and Prosperity Partnership*. Washington, D.C.: Hudson Institute, 2007.

Ángel Vela, José. "Importa PEMEX 50% de gasolina." *Reforma*, August 22, 2008, 1.

Astorga, Luis. "Drug Trafficking in Mexico: A First General Assessment." Discussion Paper No. 36, UNESCO, 1999. Also available online at http://www.unesco.org/most/astorga.htm.

Balassa, Bela, and Associates. *The Structure of Protection in Developing Countries*. International Bank for Reconstruction and Development and the Inter-American Development Bank. Baltimore, Md.: Johns Hopkins University Press, 1971.

Baylis, Kathy, and Jeffrey M. Perloff. "End Runs around Trade Restrictions: The Case of the Mexican Tomato Suspension Agreements." Giannini Foundation of Agricultural Economics. Berkley, Calif., 2005.

Becker, Gary S., Kevin M. Murphy, and Michael Grossman. "The Market for Illegal Goods: The Case of Drugs." *Journal of Political Economy* 14, no. 1 (2006): 38–60.

Beilock, Richard, and Barry E. Prentice. "A Single North American Trucking Market Experiment: The Open Prairies Proposal." Building North America: North American Transportation Competitiveness Research Council and North American Center for Transborder Studies Working Paper No. 2. Tempe, Ariz.: Arizona State University, 2007.

Bierstecker, Thomas J. "The Rebordering of North America: Implications for Conceptualizing Borders after September 11." In *The Rebordering of North America: Integration and Exclusion in a New Security Context*. Edited by Peter Andreas and Thomas J. Bierstecker, 153–65. New York: Routledge, 2003.

Brooke, James. "Tentatively, North Korea Solicits Foreign Investment and Tourism." *New York Times*, February 19, 2002, section c1.

Bueno, Gerardo M. "La estructura de la protección efectiva en México en 1960." *Demografía y economía, México* 6, no. 2 (1972): 137–205.

Califano, Joseph A. "Should Drugs Be Decriminalized? No." *British Medical Journal* 335 (November 10, 2007): 967.

Camerota, Steven A. "Immigrants in the United States, 2007: A Profile of America's Foreign-born Population." Background Paper. Center for Immigration Studies. Washington, D.C., 2007.

Carlos Baker, Juan. "TLCAN: 12 años de libre comercio." Mexico City: Secretariat of Energy, director of evaluation and monitoring of negotiation, May 2, 2006.

Castañeda, Jorge. "Call off the Immigrant Hunt." *New York Times*, December 28, 2008, WK9.

———. *ExMex: From Migrants to Immigrants*. New York: New Press, 2007.

Caulkins, Jonathan P., and Peter Reuter. "Reorienting U.S. Drug Policy." *Issues in Science and Technology* 23 (Fall 2006): 79–85.

Celia Toro, María. *Mexico's War on Drugs: Causes and Consequences*. Boulder, Colo.: Lynne Rienner Publishers, 1995.

Centro de Investigación y Docencia Económicas (CIDE) and Consejo Mexicano de Asuntos Internacionales (COMEXI). "Mexico and the World 2006: Leaders, Public Opinion, and Foreign Policy in Mexico, the United States, and Asia, a Comparative Study." Mexico City: CIDE and COMEXI, 2006.

Chabat, Jorge. "La militarización de la lucha contra el narcotráfico." In *Seguridad pública y estado en México: Análisis de algunas iniciativas*. Edited by Marcelo Bergman. Mexico City: Distribuciones Fontamara, 2007.

———. "Mexico: The Security Challenge." In *Canada and Mexico's Security in a Changing North America*. Edited by Jordi Diaz. Montreal: Queens-McGill University Press, 2007.

———. "Mexico's War on Drugs: No Margin for Maneuver." *Annals of the American Academy of Political and Social Science* 582 (2002): 134–48.

Committee to Protect Journalists (CPJ). *Attacks on the Press in 2007*. New York: CPJ, 2008.

Cook, Colleen W. "Mexico's Drug Cartels." Congressional Research Service Report for Congress, Washington, D.C., October 16, 2007.

Corchado, Alfredo. "Drug Czar Says U.S. Use Fueling Mexican Violence." *Dallas Morning News*, February 22, 2008, 1A, 6A.

Córdoba, Mayola. "Reprueba PEMEX propuesta priista." *Reforma*, July 26, 2008, 1.

Council on Foreign Relations (CFR). *Building a North American Community*. Report of an Independent Task Force Sponsored by the Council on Foreign Relations, Canadian Council of Chief Executives, and the Consejo Mexicano de Asuntos Internacionales. New York: CFR, 2005.

Crooks, Ed, and Adam Thomson. "Setback for Mexico as Service Role Is Ruled Out." *Financial Times*, April 30, 2008, 16.

Davidow, Jeffrey. *The Bear and the Porcupine: The U.S. and Mexico*. Princeton, N.J.: Markus Wiener Publishers, 2007.

Department of Homeland Security and Secretariat of Governance. "Alliance for the Mexico–U.S. Border: Progress Report, 2002–2004" (Alianza para la frontera

México–Estados Unidos: Reporte de avances, 2002–2004). Washington, D.C., and Mexico City, 2005.

DeShazo, Peter, and Johanna Mendelson Forman. "Sacar provecho al Plan Mérida." *El universal*, August 9, 2008, 14.

Deutch, John, and James R. Schlesinger. *National Security Consequences of U.S. Oil Dependency*. Task force report no. 58. New York: Council on Foreign Relations, 2006.

DeYoung, Karen. "Mexican Envoy Highly Critical of U.S. Role in Anti-Drug Effort." *Washington Post*, March 23, 2007.

Egan, Timothy. "Disorder on the Border." *New York Times*, March 29, 2008, 17.

Embassy of Mexico. "Judicial and Public Safety Reform." Factsheet. Embassy of Mexico, Washington, D.C., 2008.

Estévez, Dolia. "¿Oportunidad desperdiciada?" *Poder y negocios* 4, no. 5 (February 26, 2008): 52–55.

Farkus, Greg. "Mexico Wages Bloody War with Drug Cartels. *Voice of America News*, May 21, 2008. Radio news transcript available online at http://www.voanews.com/ english/archive/2008-05-21-voa76.cfm?moddate=2008-05-21.

Federal Motor Carrier Safety Administration (FMCSA). *NAFTA Safety Statistics database*. U.S. Department of Transportation. 2008. Available online at http:// ai.fmcsa.dot.gov/International/border.asp.

Fidler, Stephen. "Hesitant Steps over Reform Hinder Growth." *Financial Times*. Special Report: Mexico–Trade & Investment. November 17, 2008, 1.

"Five Killed in Mexico Border City amid Drug War." Reuters, March 4, 2008. Available online at http://www.reuters.com/article/worldNews/idUSN0451249520080304.

Flynn, Stephen E. 2000. "Beyond Border Control." *Foreign Affairs* 79, no. 6 (November–December): 57–68.

———. "The False Conundrum: Continental Integration versus Homeland Security." In *The Rebordering of North America: Integration and Exclusion in a New Security Context*. Edited by Peter Andreas and Thomas J. Biersteker, 110–27. New York: Routledge, 2003.

Fox, Vicente, with Rob Allyn. *Revolution of Hope: The Life, Faith, and Dreams of a Mexican President*. New York: Viking, 2007.

Fuentes, Víctor. "Pone EU auditor al Plan Mérida." *Reforma*, August 13, 2008, 3.

Gonzalez, Francisco E. *Dual Transitions from Authoritarian Rule: Institutionalized Regimes in Chile and Mexico, 1970–2000*. Baltimore, Md.: Johns Hopkins University Press, 2008.

González, Guadalupe, Susan Minushkin, Robert Y. Shapiro, and Catherine Hug. "Global Views 2004: Comparing Mexican and American Public Opinion and Foreign Policy." Mexico City and Chicago: CIDE, COMEXI, and the Chicago Council on Foreign Relations, 2004.

"Good Neighbors Make Fences." *Economist*, October 4, 2008, 25–27.

Grayson, George W. "Los Zetas: The Ruthless Army Spawned by a Mexican Drug Cartel." Philadelphia, Pa.: Foreign Policy Research Institute, 2008.

Grossman, Michael, Frank J. Chaloupka, and Kyumin Shim. "Illegal Drug Use and Public Policy." *Health Affairs* 21, no. 2 (2002): 134–45.

Gudynas, Eduardo. "Energy Diplomacy and the Crossroads in South American Unification." *IRC Americas.* Center for International Policy, Washington, D.C., July 24, 2007. Also available online at http://Americas.irc-online.org/am/4419.

Guerrero, Claudia. "Exige IP reformar PEMEX . . . y sindicato." *Reforma,* August 18, 2008, 1.

Habeeb, William Mark. *Power and Tactics in International Negotiation: How Weak Nations Bargain with Strong Nations.* Baltimore, Md.: Johns Hopkins University Press, 1988.

Haber, Stephen. "Mexico's Experiments with Bank Privatization and Liberalization, 1991–2003." *Journal of Banking and Finance* 29, nos. 8–9 (2005): 2325–53.

Harman, Danna. "Debate Far from over for Mexico's Drug Bill: Lawmakers Vowed Monday to Pass a Bill That Drops Charges for Small Amounts of Cocaine, Marijuana, and Other Drugs." *Christian Science Monitor* 8, no. 115 (May 10, 2006): 4.

Hufbauer, Gary C., and Gustavo Vega Cánovas. "Whither NAFTA: A Common Frontier." In *The Rebordering of North America: Integration and Exclusion in a New Security Context.* Edited by Peter Andreas and Thomas J. Bierstecker, 128–52. New York: Routledge, 2003.

Hufbauer, Gary C., and Jeffrey J. Schott. *NAFTA: An Assessment.* Washington, D.C.: Institute for International Economics, 1993.

———. *North American Free Trade: Issues and Recommendations.* Washington, D.C.: Institute for International Economics, 1992.

Ibarra-Yúnez, Alejandro. "Fronteras seguras y facilitación de comercio: Análisis de Economía Institucional." *Gestión y política pública* 17, no. 1 (2008): 3–33.

International Monetary Fund (IMF). *International Financial Statistics Database.* Washington, D.C.: IMF, 2008.

———. "Mexico 2007 Article IV Consultation." Washington, D.C.: IMF, 2007.

Jank, Marcos J., Géraldine Kutas, Luiz Fernando do Amaral, and André M. Nassar. "E.U. and U.S. Policies on Biofuels: Potential Impacts on Developing Countries." German Marshall Fund of the United States. Washington, D.C., 2007.

Jardón, Eduardo. "Costarán subsidios a energéticos más de 340 mil milliones de pesos." *El financiero,* July 24, 2008, 1, 4.

Jiménez, Roberto. "Cae 18% exportación de crudo." *Excelsior,* July 29, 2008, 4.

Kleiman, Mark A. R. "Dopey, Boozy, Smoky—and Stupid." *American Interest* 2, no. 3 (January–February 2007): 79–91.

Krauze, Enrique. *Mexico, Biography of Power: A History of Modern Mexico, 1810–1996.* New York: Harper Collins, 1997.

Lajous, Adrián. "Política petrolera exterior." Red Radio, Universidad de Guadalajara, Guadalajara, Mexico, March 14, 2006.

Levy, Santiago. *Progress against Poverty: Sustaining Mexico's Progresa–Oportunidades Program.* Washington, D.C.: Brookings Institution, 2006.

Lindsay, Lowell, Carla Perderzini, and Jeffrey Passel. "The Demography of Mexico/U.S. Migration." In *Mexico–U.S. Migration Management: A Binational Approach.* Edited by Susan F. Martin and Agustin Escobar Latapi. New York: Lexington Books, 2008.

Lowe, Jeffrey. "Direct Investment, 2004–2007: Detailed Historical-Cost Positions and Related Capital and Income Flows." *Survey of Current Business* 88, no. 9 (September 2008): 34–40.

Mackey, Michael W. "Report of Michael W. Mackey on the Comprehensive Evaluation of the Operations and Functions of the Fund for the Protection of Bank Savings (FOBAPROA) and Quality of Supervision of the FOBAPROA Program, 1995–1998." Submitted to the Congress of the Republic of Mexico, Mexico City, 1999.

Marshall, Ray. *Getting Immigration Reform Right.* Briefing Paper 186. Washington, D.C.: Economic Policy Institute, 2007.

Meyer, Michael C., and William L. Sherman. *The Course of Mexican History,* fifth edition. New York: Oxford University Press, 1995.

Martin, Philip. *Importing Poverty: Immigration and the Changing Face of Rural America.* New Haven, Conn.: Yale University Press, 2009.

Martin, Elizabeth. "Embracing Change on the U.S.–Mexico Border." *Foreign Service Journal* 84, no. 10 (October 2007): 33–34.

Mayer, Frederick W. *Interpreting NAFTA: The Science and Art of Political Analysis.* New York: Columbia University Press, 1998.

McQuerry, Elizabeth. "The Banking Sector Rescue in Mexico." *Economic Review* (third quarter 1999): 14–29.

Mexican Ministry of Foreign Affairs and U.S. Commission on Immigration Reform. *Migration between Mexico and the United States: Binational Study.* Mexico City and Austin, Tex.: Printed by Morgan Printing, 1997, 448.

"Mexico and the United States: A Wary Friendship." *Economist,* June 19, 2008.

"Mexico's mezzogiorno." *Economist,* November 18, 2006, 7–9.

Meyers, Deborah W. "One Face at the Border: Behind the Slogan." Migration Policy Institute, Washington, D.C., June 2005.

Morales Moreno, Isidro. *Post-NAFTA North America: Reshaping the Economic and Political Governance of a Changing Region.* New York: Palgrave Macmillan, 2008.

Muñoz, Heraldo. *A Solitary War: A Diplomat's Chronicle of the Iraq War and Its Lessons.* Golden City, Colo.: Fulcrum Publishing, 2008.

North American Steel Trade Committee (NASTC). "The Border Story—A North American Steel Industry Perspective." Canada–United States Transportation Working Group Library, Ottawa, February 2008. Available online at http://www.thetbwg.org/library-library_e.htm.

Odell, John S. "Latin American Trade Negotiations with the United States." *International Organization* 34, no. 2 (Spring 1980): 207–28.

Olson, Mancur. *The Rise and Decline of Nations: Economic Growth, Stagflation, and Social Regulation.* New Haven, Conn.: Yale University Press, 1982.

Organization for Economic Cooperation and Development (OECD). *Economic Survey of Mexico, 2007.* Paris: OECD, 2007.

————, Development Center. *Latin American Economic Outlook.* Paris: OECD, 2007.

Ortiz Mena, Antonio. "Getting to 'No': Defending against Demands in NAFTA Energy Negotiations." Documento de trabajo 126. Centro de Investigación y Docencia Económica (CIDE), Mexico City, 2005. In *Negotiating Trade: Developing Countries in the WTO and NAFTA.* Edited by John S. Odell, 177–218. Cambridge: Cambridge University Press, 2006.

Pantin, Laurence. "Se deshizo lo andado." *El norte,* November 11, 2007, 14.

Papademetriou, Demetrios, John J. Audley, Sandra Polaski, and Scott Vaughan. "NAFTA's Promise and Reality: Lessons from Mexico for the Hemisphere." Carnegie Endowment for International Peace, Washington, D.C., 2003.

Pastor, Robert A. "The Future of North America: Replacing a Bad Neighbor Policy." *Foreign Affairs* 87, no. 4 (July–August 2008): 84–98.

Paz, Octavio. *The Labyrinth of Solitude.* New York: Grove Press, 1961.

————. "Reflections: Mexico and the United States." Translated by Rachel Phillips. *The New Yorker,* September 17, 1979, 136–53.

Prebisch, Raúl. *The Economic Development of Latin America and Its Principal Problems.* New York: United Nations, Department of Economic Affairs, 1950.

Preston, Julia. "An Interpreter Speaking up for Migrants." *New York Times,* July 11, 2008, 1.

————. "270 Immigrants Sent to Prison in Federal Push." *New York Times,* May 24, 2008, 1.

Puryear, Jeffrey. "Reform in Mexico Forces Debate on Sales of Teaching Positions." *Latin American Advisor,* November 24, 2008, 3.

Quintana, Enrique. "Aumentarán más diesel y gasolina en 2009." *Reforma,* August 18, 2008, 6.

Raymond, Lee, and others. *Facing the Hard Truths about Energy: A Comprehensive View to 2030 of Global Oil and Natural Gas.* Washington, D.C.: National Petroleum Council, 2007.

Reid, Michael. "Time to Wake Up." *Economist,* November 18, 2006, 3–5.

Reuter, Peter, and David Ronfeldt. "Quest for Integrity: The Mexican–U.S. Drug Issue in the 1980s." Special issue: "Drug Trafficking Research Update." *Journal of Interamerican Studies and World Affairs* 34, no. 3 (Fall 1992): 89–153.

Riding, Alan. *Distant Neighbors: A Portrait of the Mexicans.* New York: Vintage, 1984.

Rivero, Arturo, and Laura Carrillo. "Tienen mas trabajo . . . ¡en EU!" *Reforma,* July 25, 2008.

Roberts, Adams. "Special Report on Migration." *Economist,* January 5, 2008.

Roig-Franzia, Manuel. "Anti-Drug Assistance Approved for Mexico: U.S. Lawmakers Responded to Counterparts' Objections." *Washington Post,* June 28, 2008, A08.

————. "Apparent Mexican Winner Attacks Border Wall." *Washington Post,* July 8, 2006.

————. "Drug Trade Tyranny on the Border." *Washington Post,* March 16, 2008, A01.

————. "Mexican Leader Sees Bias in U.S. Politicking: Stop Disparaging Migrants, Calderón Says." *Washington Post,* November 15, 2007.

Roumasset, James, and Min Min Thaw. "The Economics of Prohibition: Price,

Consumption, and Enforcement Expenditures during Alcohol Prohibition." *Hawaii Reporter* (2003). Available online at http://www.hawaiireporter.com/file. aspx?Guid=cf0541b8-adda-4c54-ab20-f72fe6f9a3aa.

Rubio, Luis. "NAFTA and Mexico." The Perspectives on the Americas series. Center for Hemispheric Policy, University of Miami, 2008.

———. "Sacralización." *Reforma*, July 27, 2008, 17.

Salinas de Gortari, Carlos. *México, un paso difícil a la modernidad*. Barcelona, Spain: Plaza y Janés, 2000.

Schettino, Macario. *Cien años de confusión: México en el siglo XX*. Madrid: Santillana Ediciones Generales and Taurus Publishing, 2007.

Schott, Jeffrey J. "Trade Negotiations among NAFTA Partners." In *Requiem or Revival: The Promise of North American Economic Integration*. Edited by Isabel Studer and Carol Wise, 76–88. Washington, D.C.: Brookings Institution, 2007.

Secretariat of Energy (SENER). "Perspectiva de mercado de petróleo crudo, 2007–2012." Mexico City: SENER, 2007.

Selee, Andrew. "More Than Neighbors: An Overview of Mexico and U.S. Mexican Relations." Woodrow Wilson Center, Washington, D.C., 2007.

Serrano, Mónica. "Bordering on the Impossible: U.S.–Mexico Security Relations after 9/11." In *The Rebordering of North America: Integration and Exclusion in a New Security Context*. Edited by Peter Andreas and Thomas Biersecker, 46–67. New York: Routledge, 2003.

Skerry, Peter. "How Not to Build a Fence." *Foreign Policy* (September–October 2006).

Smith, Adam. *An Inquiry into the Nature and Causes of the Wealth of Nations*. New York: Random House, 1937.

Storrs, K. Larry. "Mexico's Counter-Narcotics Efforts under Fox, December 2000 to October 2004." Congressional Research Service report for the U.S. Congress, Washington, D.C., November 2004.

U.S. Census Bureau, Foreign Trade Division. *Related Party Trade, 2007*. Available online at http://www.census.gov/foreign-trade/Press-Release/2007pr/aip/related_party/.

U.S. Department of Homeland Security. *The Mexico–U.S. Border Partnership: Progress Report 2002–2004*. Washington, D.C.: U.S. Department of Homeland Security / Secretaría de Gobernación, 2005.

Vega Cánovas, Gustavo. "De la protección a la aperatura commercial." In *Una historia contemporánea de México*. Edited by Ilan Bizberg and Lorenzo Meyer. Mexico City: Editorial Oceano y El Colegio de México, 2009.

Verini, James. "Arming the Drug Wars." *Condé Nast Portfolio*, June 16, 2008. Available online at http://www.portfolio.com/news-markets/international-news/portfolio/2008/06/16/Examining-the-US-Mexico-Gun-Trade/.

Verrastro, Frank. "The United States." In *Energy Cooperation in the Western Hemisphere: Benefits and Impediments*. Edited by Sidney Weintraub, Annette Hester, and Veronica Prado, 41–69. Washington, D.C.: Center for Strategic and International Studies (CSIS) Press, 2007.

Villa, Juan C. "Border Transportation Studies Review: Final Report." Texas Transportation Institute, Texas A&M University System, College Station, August 2005.

———. "Transaction Costs in the Transportation Sector and Infrastructure in North America: Exploring Harmonization of Standards." Report from the International Trade and Industry Unit of ECLAC/Mexico. United Nations Economic Commission on Latin America and the Caribbean (ECLAC), August 2007.

Von Bertrab, Hermann. *Negotiating NAFTA: A Mexican Envoy's Account*. Washington, D.C.: CSIS Press, 1997.

"A Wary Friendship." *Economist*, June 21, 2008, 49–50.

Watkins, Ralph. "The China Challenge to Manufacturing in Mexico." Lecture given at George Mason University, Fairfax, Va., April 28, 2007.

Weintraub, Sidney. "Development Aid Can Ease Illegal Immigration." *Financial Times*, April 18, 2005, 19.

———. *Financial Decision-making in Mexico: To Bet a Nation*. Pittsburgh, Pa.: University of Pittsburgh Press, 2000.

———. *Free Trade between Mexico and the United States*. Washington, D.C.: Brookings Institution Press, 1984.

———. "Scoring Free Trade." *Current History* 103, no. 670 (February 2004): 56–60.

———, ed. *NAFTA's Impact on North America: The First Decade*. Washington, D.C.: CSIS Press, 2004.

Weintraub, Sidney, and Rafael Fernández de Castro. "Mexico." In *Energy Cooperation in the Western Hemisphere: Benefits and Impediments*. Edited by Sidney Weintraub, Annette Hester, and Veronica Prado. Washington, D.C.: CSIS Press, 2007.

Weintraub, Sidney, Annette Hester, and Veronica Prado, eds. *Energy Cooperation in the Western Hemisphere: Benefits and Impediments*. Washington, D.C.: CSIS Press, 2007.

Wise, Carol. "Unfulfilled Promise: Economic Convergence Under NAFTA." In *Requiem or Revival: The Promise of North American Integration*. Edited by Isabel Studer and Carol Wise. Washington, D.C.: Brookings Institution, 2007.

Wolf, Martin. "Welcome to the New World of Runaway Energy Demand." *Financial Times*, November 14, 2007, 11.

World Bank. *World Development Indicators*. Washington, D.C.: World Bank, 2008.

Zahniser, Steven, and William Coyle. "U.S.-Mexico Corn Trade during the NAFTA Era: New Twists to an Old Story." Economic Research Service, U.S. Department of Agriculture, Washington, D.C., May 2004.

Zartman, William. "The Structuralist Dilemma in Negotiation." Research Group in International Security, Montreal, January 1997.

Index

agriculture: drug crops in, 68–69, 74–75, 77–78; immigrant labor in U.S., 106–7, 109–10, 113; Mexico's, 18–19; in NAFTA negotiations, 32, 37–38
Aguilar Zinser, Adolfo, 1–2, 142n1
Alba, Francisco, 99
Alden, Edward, 118
Álvarez Macháin, Humberto, 73, 79–80
Argentina, 19
arms sales, and violence in drug trafficking, 72–73, 81, 148n37
Asia, depending on exports for economic growth, 26–27
Aspe, Pedro, 50
automobile industry, 45, 60, 90

Baker, James, 31
Banco Obrero, 46, 60
Bank Fund for the Protection of Savings (Fondo Bancario de Protección al Ahorro, FOBAPROA), 53–54, 61, 63
Bank of Mexico (Banco de México), 53–54
banks, Mexican: foreign investment in, 47, 52; foreign ownership of, 46, 52–53, 58, 133–34; opening of private, 59; reprivatization of, 48–49, 61, 146n5, 146n17; in rescue plan for economic crisis, 54, 62–63, 146n5; stability of, 50, 59; structural changes in, 55
BBVA bank, 57
Becker, Gary, 67
Beltran Leyva Organization, 71
Bertrab, Hermann von, 35
border: Canada-U.S., 117; common frontier proposals for, 43, 119; control measures at, 129; crossing times at, 117–18, 120–21, 153n7, 153n8; dangers of crossing, 104–5, 112, 114, 130; definition of, 128; dependency and dominance issues at, 127–28; effects of U.S.-Mexican trucking dispute on, 123–24; efforts to move actions away from, 119–20, 129–30; environmental issues at, 128, 138; inefficiencies at, 120, 137; Mexico's eco-nomic growth occurring around, 11; moving actions away from, 153n12; traffic across, 116–17; vehicle inspections in Operation Intercept, 68, 77–78
border fence, 114–15, 130, 137; Mexican opposition to, 106, 126, 128, 132, 134, 139; motives for building, 105, 126
border security, 4, 9, 106–7, 112–14, 137; efforts to move actions away from actual border, 119–20; immigration conflated with, 118, 132; increasing bottleneck due to, 36, 117
bracero program, 11, 40, 110
Brady, Nicholas, 28
Brazil, 19, 85–87, 91, 94, 142n20
Buckley, William, 66
Bueno, Gerardo M., 28
Bush, George H. W., 31, 41–42, 78
Bush, George W., 43, 96; Mérida meeting with Calderón, 7, 74, 76, 134; on migration issues, 105, 113–15, 130, 135; on NAFTA, 42–43; questionable election of, 141n4; on U.S.-Mexican trucking dispute, 39, 122; war on drugs under, 66, 81
business tax, added under Calderón, 14–15

Calderón Hinojosa, Felipe, 13, 20, 43, 99; assertiveness with U.S., 106, 134; criticizing border fence, 114–15, 126, 128, 134; criticizing U.S. contribution to war on drugs, 74, 76, 134; in domestic politics, 21, 22, 142n19; on economic growth to reduce emigration, 101, 108; economic policies under, 14–15, 85; fighting police corruption, 69–70, 75; Mérida Initiative by, 7, 81; on migration issues, 106, 135; proposing changes in Pemex, 87–88, 92, 96
Califano, Joseph, 67
Calvo Doctrine, 57
Camarena, Enrique, 73, 78
Canada, 155n3; free trade agreements of, 31, 127, 144n14 (*see also* North American Free

165

pilot program for NAFTA provisions on, 39, 43, 130, 135–36; U.S. agreements with Canada, 155n3; U.S. violation of NAFTA provisions on, 38–39, 120–27, 129–30, 132, 135, 137, 154n29

"Unfulfilled Promise" (Wise), 33–34
United Nations, Mexican opposition to Iraq war in, 6, 134
United States: aggressiveness toward Mexico, 131–32; foreign-born residents of, 98; interventions in Mexico, 27; Mexican-born population in, 5, 102; myth of energy independence in, 89–90, 150n25; negotiations with less-powerful nations, 8–9; not prioritizing relations with Mexico, 133, 139; power of, 2–3, 8
U.S.-Mexico Smart Border Accord, 129
US Visit, 129

Vargas Llosa, Mario, 20
Vega Cánovas, Gustavo, 29–30, 119
Veracruz, naval occupation of, 2
Villa, Juan Carlos, 120, 124

violence, in drug trafficking, 59, 70–71, 76, 148n29, 148n37; U.S. blame for, 72–73, 81, 139
Volcker, Paul, 29

Walters, John, 71–72
war on drugs. *See* drugs, war on
Wilson, Pete, 112
Wilson, Woodrow, 2
Wise, Carol, 33–34
Wolf, Martin, 90
World Bank, 57

Zapatista National Revolutionary Army (Ejercito Zapatista de Liberación Nacional, EZLN), 49
Zartman, William, 8–9
Zedillo Ponce de León, Ernesto, 42, 80–81; bank rescue plan of, 54, 63; in domestic politics, 21, 49–50; economic policies of, 12, 30, 51, 95
Zetas, 71, 76. *See also* drug trafficking: Mexican cartels in